THE UNIFICATION OF ITALY

Graham Darby
Series editor: Christopher Culpin

Longman

Edinburgh Gate
Harlow, Essex

CONTENTS

PART ONE

INTRODUCTION

The (so-called) unification of Italy was a remarkable event which took contemporaries completely by surprise. Palmerston thought it 'miraculous as no one in his senses or in his dreams could have anticipated [it]', and Gladstone described it as 'among the great marvels of our time'. Subsequently, Italian historians set out to generate national feeling by claiming that unification had not been a sudden event but was in fact the culmination of a long-term evolutionary process, part of an unfolding grand design – part of a *Risorgimento* (a national resurgence). This approach tended to emphasise Italian rather than foreign contributions to unification and played down the differences between the main players. Much of this was a myth, but the idea of progress towards a nationalist solution to Italian disunity was also favoured by British historians at the turn of the century, and it dominated interpretation for some time thereafter. However, since the Second World War, and largely due to the work of the British historian, Denis Mack Smith, unification has come to be portrayed as the rather sudden accidental by-product of international power politics, of war and diplomacy, an event in which greed and jealousy among the main players was more in evidence than cooperation and understanding. In short, we have in some respects reverted to the position taken by those contemporaries mentioned at the beginning: it was a surprise – it was an accident.

It is the purpose of this book to help the student pick his or her way through the events of Italian history between 1815 and 1870, peel away the layers of myth and make sense of not only what happened but why it happened. As you go through this book, these are some of the key questions that you ought to be asking:

◢ Was the unification of Italy a long-term evolutionary process? In short, was there a *Risorgimento*?

◢ Was the unification the result of nationalist fervour?

◢ What were the roles of the major players – Napoleon III, Cavour and Garibaldi – and who made the decisive contribution?

◢ Was unification an accident, an aberration – mainly the result of factors outside Italy?

◢ Was Italy unified at all, or was it simply conquered by one of its states?

Chronology

1814–15	Collapse of the Napoleonic regimes in Italy; Restoration of the old rulers by the Congress of Vienna
1820	Revolutions in southern Italy (Mezzogiorno) and Sicily
1821	Revolution in Turin, conspiracy in Milan
1831	Revolutions in central Italy
	Mazzini's Young Italy founded
1843	Publication of Vincenzo Gioberti's *On the Moral and Civil Primacy of the Italians*
1844	Publication of Cesare Balbo's *Of the Hopes of Italy*
1846	Election of Pius IX (Giovanni Maria Mastai-Ferretti: Pope 1846–78)
1848	12 January: Revolution in Palermo
	22–4 February: Revolution in Paris
	13 March: Revolution in Vienna
	18–22 March: Austrians driven out of Milan (the *Cinque Giornate*)
	21–3 March: Revolution in Venice
	23 March: Charles Albert (King of Sardinia 1831–49) grants constitution
	29 April: Pius IX condemns the war against Austria
	15 May: Royalist coup in Naples
	25 July: Piedmontese army defeated at the battle of Custoza
	21 October: Collapse of moderate government in Tuscany
	15 November: Murder of Pellegrino Rossi in Rome
	24 November: Pius IX flees to Gaeta
1849	8 February: Proclamation of the Roman Republic
	23 March: Piedmontese army defeated by the Austrians at the battle of Novara

	Abdication of Charles Albert – succeeded by Victor Emmanuel II (King of Sardinia 1849–61; King of Italy 1861–78)
	3 July: Fall of the Roman Republic
	7 August: Fall of the Venetian Republic
1851	Free trade legislation in Piedmont
	2 December: Louis Napoleon's coup in France
1852	November: Camillo Benso di Cavour (1810–61) first appointed Prime Minister in Piedmont
	2 December: Louis Napoleon assumes title of Emperor of the French
1853(–6)	Crimean War
1855	Conflict with Church over legislation to suppress monasteries in Piedmont
1857	July: Founding of the Italian National Society
1858	January: Attempt on life of Napoleon III by Felice Ursini (Italian nationalist)
	July: Secret meeting at Plombières
1859	19–23 April: Austrian ultimatum to Turin
	4 June: Battle of Magenta
	'Revolutions' in the Romagna, Tuscany, Modena and Parma
	24 June: Battle of Solferino
	11 July: Armistice of Villafranca
1860	March: Plebiscites in Tuscany, Emilia, Nice and Savoy
	April: Nice and Savoy ceded to France
	4 April: Insurrection near Palermo
	5 May: Garibaldi's Thousand sail from Genoa
	11 May: Garibaldi's landing at Marsala
	30 May: Fall of Palermo
	7 September: Garibaldi enters Naples
	29 September: Piedmontese army invades Papal States to stop Garibaldi's advance
	21 October: Annexation of Naples
	25 October: Meeting between Garibaldi and Victor Emmanuel at Teano
	5 November: Annexation of Sicily
1861	Beginning of the civil war ('brigandage') in the south
1862	August: Garibaldi relaunches the March on Rome
	September: Aspromonte
1866	Prusso-Austrian War:
	3 July: Battle of Königgrätz
	War against Austria
	Italy acquires Venice
1867	Nationalist invasion of Papal States halted at Mentana
1870	1 September: Prussia defeats Napoleon III at Sedan
	20 September: Italian troops enter Rome through the Porta Pia

Chronological survey of the period

1 Restoration and repressed uprisings, 1815–31

In 1815 Italy was simply a geographical expression; it had not existed as a unified country since the early Middle Ages. As you can see from Figure 1, it consisted of a number of small, relatively weak states, and the people tended to owe their loyalty to their locality. There was little sense of nationalism (a sense of patriotism, of belonging to a common Italian nation) in the peninsula and only a few envisaged unification (the consolidation of all the states into a single state).

After Napoleon, many of the old states of Italy were restored and Austria was given either direct or indirect control over a number of them. Italy was thus fragmented and dominated by Austria.

Dissatisfaction with restored government among the educated few manifested itself in uprisings in Naples and Piedmont in 1820–1, and in Modena, Parma and the Romagna in 1831. However, in all these cases the repressive hand of Prince Metternich and the Austrian army ensured that native aspirations were soon extinguished.

2 The growth of Italian identity, 1831–47

The growth of Italian identity can be most easily summed up by the three 'p's – the people, the Pope and Piedmont – reflected in the writings of Mazzini, Gioberti and Balbo. All three writers envisaged some sort of unified Italy – Mazzini a republic brought about by a revolution of the people, Gioberti a confederation headed up by the Pope, and Balbo a federation created by Piedmont which would expel the Austrians. All three models for unification were drawn up in the 1830s and 1840s; all three were embraced by a very small educated minority; and all three were totally unrealistic. However, they did reflect a growing wish for Italian independence from Austrian domination which was to manifest itself in 1848–9.

3 The revolutions of 1848–9

The aim of the uprisings of 1848–9 was to expel the Austrians rather than to unify Italy, but in each case the Italians failed. The lesson was that the Italians were no match for the Austrian army; they would need outside help. Nevertheless, national consciousness was raised,

Figure 1 Italy in 1815

and Piedmont rather than the Pope became the focus for future
aspirations as Pius IX had set himself against change.

4 Cavour and Napoleon III: the 1850s

Cavour was Prime Minister of Piedmont from 1852. He did not
envisage Italian unification. His main aim was to expel the Austrians
from Italy, extend Piedmont and create a north Italian kingdom. To

this end he courted Napoleon III for many years, but when Napoleon did finally respond in 1858, it was on the latter's terms and quite by chance. It is clear that despite his central role, Cavour was not in a position to dictate events – but he did take his opportunities.

5 The unification process, 1859–61

Napoleon's war against Austria did not go according to plan, but by exploiting instability in the central duchies (Tuscany, Parma and Modena, as well as the Romagna – see Figure 1) and by giving up Nice and Savoy to France, Cavour was able, by March 1860, to achieve an enlarged Piedmont, his original aim.

And then, out of the blue, Garibaldi, a disciple of Mazzini, forced Cavour to embrace unification. Garibaldi himself actually believed in unification and set out to achieve it. Taking advantage of an uprising in Sicily, he landed there, conquered the island and then went on to conquer the Kingdom of Naples on the mainland. It was an incredible achievement, a saga so far-fetched it resembles fiction! Garibaldi's threat to the Pope forced Cavour to march south, conquering much of the Papal States and linking up the northern Italian kingdom with Garibaldi's conquests. Garibaldi then generously handed over to King Victor Emmanuel of Piedmont. In 1861 the latter was proclaimed King of Italy.

6 Postscript – Venetia 1866 and Rome 1870

Venetia was still occupied by the Austrians and Rome by the French. Both of these territories came to Italy in somewhat inglorious episodes courtesy of the Prussian Minister, Bismarck. Successful Prussian wars against both Austria and France enabled Victor Emmanuel to complete the process of unification by 1870, though arguably Italy had been Piedmontised rather than unified. What had been hailed as a miracle and a marvel was soon viewed with disillusion and disappointment.

Giuseppe Mazzini, *1805–72*

The foremost Italian nationalist, Mazzini was born in Genoa and trained to be a lawyer. He founded Young Italy in 1831, a movement dedicated to the unification of a republican Italy. However, it had little impact beyond publicity though an important convert was Garibaldi. Mazzini briefly took charge of the Roman Republic in 1849 but played no role in the actual unification from 1859. He spent most of his life in exile and was disillusioned with the Italy that eventually came into being. He was subsequently credited as 'father of the nation' and hailed as a prophet.

Giuseppe Garibaldi, *1807–82*

Born in Nice, Garibaldi was a merchant seaman when he met Mazzini and became a committed nationalist. He spent some time in exile in South America before returning to Italy during the 1848 Revolutions, where in 1849 he commanded the garrison of the Roman Republic. After another spell of exile he returned and was actively involved in the war against Austria. It was his remarkable expedition to Sicily and then Naples in 1860 that really brought about unification. By now a committed monarchist, he handed over his conquests to Victor Emmanuel but became disillusioned with the new Italy. He led two unsuccessful expeditions against the Pope in Rome in 1862 and 1867. A man of immense charisma, Garibaldi enjoyed superstar status in his day, and crowds filled Trafalgar Square when he came to London in 1864.

Victor Emmanuel II, *1820–78*

The first King of Italy, Victor Emmanuel became King of Piedmont-Sardinia in 1849 after his father abdicated, and appointed Cavour as Prime Minister in 1852. He pushed for Piedmontese participation in the Crimean War and actively encouraged the unification process, which he saw as Piedmontese expansion. His coarse manners gave him the common touch, and Garibaldi's respect for him was a significant factor in creating the new state. He was proclaimed King of Italy in 1861. He added Venetia in 1866 and Rome in 1870. Though devious and cunning, he lacked application and was prepared to tolerate the constitution.

Count Camillo Benso di Cavour, *1810–61*

Born in Turin, Cavour visited England in the 1830s, founded the newspaper *Il Risorgimento* and the Bank of Turin in 1847, served in d'Azeglio's government and succeeded him as Prime Minister in 1852, a position he was to hold (excepting a six-month break in 1859) until his premature death in 1861. He was not a nationalist but worked hard to expand Piedmont at the expense of Austria. His deal with Napoleon III in 1858 set in motion the process that led to unification. He worked to include the central duchies in the new kingdom in 1860, and invaded the Papal States to pre-empt Garibaldi, thereby inadvertently unifying Italy. He was devious and cunning but nevertheless successful.

Napoleon III, *1808–73*

Napoleon III was the nephew of the great Napoleon. He spent much of his early life in exile, some of it in Italy. After the 1848 Revolutions he was elected President of the Second Republic in France. In 1851, after a coup, he dissolved the constitution and a year later proclaimed the Second Empire, styling himself Emperor Napoleon III. An attempted assassination in 1858 prompted him to help Piedmont drive the Austrians out of Italy, but the war was only partially successful and did not achieve his aims (1859). In 1860 he obtained Nice and Savoy from Piedmont but kept troops in Rome to protect the Pope until 1870, when they were withdrawn to fight the Prussians in a war that brought about his downfall. His contribution to the process of unification was crucial but inadvertent (i.e. the outcome was not his intention) and he received little gratitude or recognition for it.

Pope Pius IX, *1792–1878*

Born Giovanni Mastai-Ferretti, Pius IX was pope from 1846 to 1878, the longest pontificate in history. Initially he was thought to be a liberal as he passed a number of reforms; however, his experience in the 1848 Revolutions, when he went briefly into exile, turned him into an arch-conservative and set the Church against change. He opposed the unification process, lost much of his lands in 1860 and Rome itself in 1870. Styling himself the 'prisoner of the Vatican', he refused to recognise the new Italy and called upon all Catholics to do the same.

THE RULERS OF THE STATES

The Two Sicilies
Ferdinand I 1759–1825*
Francis I 1825–30
Ferdinand II 1830–59
Francis II 1859–61

Piedmont-Sardinia
Victor Emmanuel I 1802–21*
Charles Felix 1821–31
Charles Albert 1831–49
Victor Emmanuel II 1849–61
(Hereafter styled King of Italy)

Papal States
Pius VII 1800–23*
Leo XII 1823–9
Pius VIII 1829–30
Gregory XVI 1831–46
Pius IX 1846–78

Tuscany
Ferdinand III 1790–1824*
Leopold II 1824–59

Parma
Maria Luisa 1815–47
Charles II 1847–9
Charles III 1849–54
Maria Luisa 1854–9†

Modena
Francis IV 1815–46
Francis V 1846–59

* Rule interrupted by French occupation.
† Regent

PART TWO

CHAPTER ONE

WAS ITALY MERELY A 'GEOGRAPHICAL EXPRESSION'?

Objectives

⏶ To determine whether or not Italians felt a common identity

⏶ To explain Italy's political fragmentation

⏶ To explain Austria's dominance of the peninsula

⏶ To profile the various states of Italy

⏶ To consider the unrest of 1820–1 and 1831

⏶ To examine the nationalism of Mazzini and the writings of Balbo and Gioberti.

What did the Austrian Chancellor, Prince Metternich, mean when he said this? Of course he meant that Italy did not exist as a political entity, but more than that he was suggesting that there was no nationalist feeling in Italy, no sense of common identity, no desire by the people to unite and rule themselves. In short, he argued that the Italians were not a single people and did not want to be. And of course he said this to remind others that the legal settlement of Vienna was unalterable. Yet he had a point. Italy had been fragmented into a number of smaller states since the collapse of the Ostrogothic kingdom in the sixth century. Despite a common cultural and linguistic heritage, it is probably true to say that Italians were Neapolitans, Tuscans or Sicilians first and Italians only second. There was little sense of nationalism in the peninsula and only a few people envisaged its unification. The family, the locality, the region came first. The vast majority of the Italian population (which numbered about 20 million in 1815, 25 million by 1861) were peasants who had no contact with political ideas, while illiteracy and widespread use of dialect (as late as 1870 only 2 per cent of the population spoke Italian) make it impossible to speak of 'cultural nationalism' except in relation to the narrow elite of propertied and professional classes (less than 2 per cent). Even among that group there was little consensus over Italy's political future beyond vague hopes of independence from Austrian domination.

◢ Source

... and consider the six focal centres of activity which control the destiny of the eighteen million inhabitants of Italy: Turin, Milan, Modena, Florence, Rome and Naples. You do not need telling that these very different peoples are very far from forming a homogeneous nation. Bergamo detests Milan, which is likewise execrated by Novara and Pavia; whereas your Milanese himself, being fully preoccupied with keeping a good table and acquiring a warm overcoat against the winter, hates nobody; for hatred would merely disturb the unruffled serenity of his pleasures. Florence, which in days gone by so bitterly abhorred Siena, now is so reduced to impotence that she has no strength for loathing left; yet, allowing for these two exceptions, I search in vain to discover a third; each city detests its neighbours, and is mortally detested in return. It follows therefore that our rulers have no difficulty in the fulfilment of their aim: divide et imperes [divide in order to rule].

An army officer, Cavaletti, reported by Stendhal in **Rome, Naples and Florence**
(originally written in 1817; this version 1826) quoted in Derek Beales,
The Risorgimento and the Unification of Italy (Longman, 1981)

Political geography

Even geographically Italy was divided and fragmented – divided from east to west by the Apennines, and divided north from south by climate. 'The fertile plains of ... the north with their regular rain fall contrasted sharply with the dry hot malarial flood-prone south' (Shreeves, 1984).

Moreover, Italy had been fragmented, politically weakened and dominated by outsiders since the early medieval era. The peninsula had been dominated by the Spanish branch of the Habsburg family in the sixteenth and seventeenth centuries, and then to a lesser extent by the Austrian Habsburgs and the Spanish Bourbons in the eighteenth. *Ancien régime* Italy was swept away after Napoleon Bonaparte invaded in the name of revolutionary France in 1796. In 1805 he styled himself King of Italy. French influence proved to be considerable. The establishment of constitutions, the codification of laws, the modernisation of the bureaucracies, the reduction of Church influence, the abolition of feudalism – all these characteristics of French rule created new sources of social mobility ('new men' got a taste of political influence) and political tension. Land redistribution penalised the poor, weakened the Church, strengthened the wealthy landowners and created a legacy of rural conflict. Moreover, the disruption created by foreign occupation, together with frequent alterations of territorial frontiers, undermined the legitimacy of the *ancien régime* governments. The old certainties were swept away – the result was instability. However, it has been suggested that the most significant legacy of French occupation, which ended with the Restoration in 1815, was a dislike of foreigners, and that in itself required some measure of national self-identity.

KEY TERM

Ancien régime (French for the 'old order') is a term used to describe the structure of government and society in Europe prior to the French Revolution in 1789. In particular, it refers to monarchical rule and a society in which an elite of aristocracy and clergy enjoyed a privileged existence compared to that of the ordinary people.

What was restored at the ***Restoration*** in 1815? Italy after 1815 reflected the interests of the victorious European powers. The main aim of the peace makers at Vienna was to prevent Italy from being vulnerable to another French invasion. This was to be done by putting the peninsula under the control of the Austrian Habsburgs and by creating an enlarged buffer state, Piedmont, on the French border. To some extent the clock was turned back to the eighteenth century in that many of the old states were recreated and the ruling dynasties, aristocracy and priests returned. However, pragmatism rather than legitimacy determined the outcome and the *ancien régime* was not fully restored – republics, for instance, were quite out of fashion as they were of course associated with revolutionary republican France.

KEY TERM

Restoration simply refers to the period after 1815 when many of the ruling houses deposed by revolutionary France were restored after Napoleon's downfall.

State	Ruling family	Population	Principal cities
Lombardy-Venetia	Austrian Habsburgs	5 million	Milan, Venice
Grand Duchy of Tuscany	Habsburg-Lorraine	1.275 million	Florence
Duchy of Modena*	Habsburg-Este	800,000	Modena
Duchy of Parma†	Habsburg		Parma
Kingdom of Two Sicilies (i.e. Naples and Sicily)	Bourbon	7.5 million	Naples, Palermo
Papal States	Pope	2.5 million	Rome, Bologna
Piedmont (i.e. Sardinia, Piedmont, Genoa, Nice and Savoy)	Savoy	3.8 million	Turin

* The duchies of Massa and Carrara did not become part of Modena until 1829.
† The Duchy of Lucca was ruled by a branch of the Bourbons until 1847 when it became part of Tuscany; the Bourbons took over Parma.
Population figures are for 1830 and are of course approximate.

Figure 2 The Restoration states

As you can see from Figure 2, the key to Habsburg control was direct rule over Lombardy and Venetia, which were incorporated into the Austrian Empire. Lombardy, as the Duchy of Milan, had been controlled by the Habsburg family since 1540, so this was not an entirely new departure; however, Venetia (with its capital Venice) had long been an independent republic (the Republic of St Mark). In addition, the Austrians had police supervision in Parma (and Piacenza), which was granted to Napoleon's wife, the Habsburg princess Maria Luisa (the duchy reverted to a branch of the Bourbon family on her death in 1847). The Habsburgs also had other relatives in the Grand Duchy of Tuscany, the capital of which was Florence, where Grand Duke Ferdinand III was restored; and in Modena, which was ruled by Duke Francis IV. Pope Pius VII was restored to the Papal States and the Bourbons were restored in Naples, which King Ferdinand I now ruled as the King of the Two Sicilies (so titled from 1816).

Ferdinand signed a permanent defensive alliance with Austria which granted the right of intervention, and the Pope allowed the Austrian army to maintain a permanent garrison in Ferrara. The only state to be relatively independent was the Kingdom of Sardinia, which was usually known as Piedmont and consisted of Savoy-Sardinia with the addition of what had been the Genoese Republic (Liguria). This kingdom was ruled from Turin by Victor Emmanuel I of the House of Savoy (see Figure 1 on page 7).

Italy, then, was complicated, and it is essential that students grasp the political geography of the peninsula in order to appreciate both its political fragmentation and its dominance by Austria. Neither of these factors made unification a likely future outcome.

The Restoration states

Lombardy-Venetia

Lombardy-Venetia was the second most populous of the Italian states and the most prosperous (with twice the national income of Piedmont in 1830), but this had more to do with the efforts of the people than the Austrian government. Lombardy fared better than Venetia (the port of Venice was not developed by either the Lombards or Austrians), enjoying considerable economic growth between 1815 and 1848 based on silk exports and agricultural production. Communications were good (though the Austrians were slow to develop railways), and compulsory free primary education meant that the literacy rate of 46 per cent (1861) was the highest in the peninsula. The two states were treated equally as a unit and ruled by an Austrian viceroy, who had residences in both Milan and Venice. Austrian rule was resented because of high taxation (Austria drew one-third of its revenue from Lombardy even though it represented only one-sixth of the Empire's population), conscription, the Austrian judicial system, Austrian officials, the use of the German language, heavy-handed censorship and backward protectionist commercial policy. Moreover, the state was overpopulated and foodstuffs had to be imported. Dissatisfaction was widespread.

Piedmont-Sardinia

The third most populous Italian state, Piedmont had been ruled by the House of Savoy since 1559. The Dukes had inherited the island of Sardinia in 1720 with the title of 'King'. Sardinia itself was a little populated and economically undeveloped island with a very low literacy rate (10 per cent in 1861). Piedmont was also relatively poor (agriculture was backward and roads were inadequate) though it did have an army, a diplomatic service and a bureaucracy – all traits of a monarchical system of government. There were, however, a large number of peasant proprietors (800,000) and a silk industry. Although the Restoration led to the abolition of conscription and taxes, the destruction of all evidence of the French period was a backward step. Internal customs barriers were re-erected, as were external ones. The addition of the Republic of Genoa – much resented by the Genoese – moved Piedmont's centre of gravity further into the Italian peninsula.

The urban and middle classes – bankers, merchants, small landowners, lawyers, civil servants and teachers – became increasingly dissatisfied with the government and demanded a constitution. In short, Piedmont was a combination of negatives and positives. However, it has recently been argued that Charles Albert's financial, economic and educational reforms of the 1840s began the process of change that was to transform the Piedmontese economy in the 1850s. Moreover, Piedmont was at least relatively independent.

The Grand Duchy of Tuscany

Tuscany had enjoyed a distinguished history and the language of Florence would provide the model for the national language. The Grand Duchy was densely populated and had its own port, Leghorn. The rule of Ferdinand III was generally enlightened and sensible, as was that of his son, Ferdinand IV, who retained popular affection until 1859. Tuscany was untouched by the upheavals of 1820–1 and 1831. The Tuscan economy had elements of strength (export of olive oil and wine, a small-scale textile industry and early railway development) and weakness (the countryside was generally unproductive and industry was too small-scale).

The duchies of Parma and Modena

These duchies were relatively small and economically poor. The moderate rule of Maria Luisa in Parma contrasted with the more reactionary approach of Francis IV in Modena (beards and moustaches were banned). After Maria Luisa's death in 1847, Parma reverted to a branch of the Spanish Bourbons who gave up Lucca to Tuscany (and did not retain the Duchess's popularity). The economies were almost exclusively agricultural.

The Papal States

The Papal States actually consisted of seventeen provinces but it is customary to refer to four regions: the area around Rome (Italy's second largest city) known as Lazio or the Patrimony of St Peter; the area to the north, Umbria; across the Apennines, the area known as the Marches; and to the north of that, the area known as the Legations (or Romagna) consisting of the important cities of Bologna and Ferrara. The people were poor, particularly around Rome (though the city itself was quite prosperous), crime was rife and the literacy rate was only a meagre 16 per cent (1861). The only genuine industrial centre was Bologna, where silk and hemp were produced. It was in the cities of the Legations that a politically aware (and politically dissatisfied) middle class emerged. The Papacy itself had lost its influence as an international force in the eighteenth century; however, Napoleon's imprisonment of Pius VII had turned Pius into something of a martyr and at the Restoration his reputation was high. The comparative enlightenment of his pontificate was followed by his successors' repressive rule which led to revolution in 1831. It was only with the election of Pius IX in 1846 that optimism returned.

The Kingdom of the Two Sicilies

The kingdom, more commonly known as the Kingdom of Naples, consisted of the whole of southern Italy and the island of Sicily. It was the most populous state and the city of Naples the most populous city (perhaps 400,000); Palermo, the capital of Sicily, was the third most populous city. The kingdom had been ruled by a branch of the Spanish Bourbons since 1734. The King resided in Naples and ruled Sicily through a viceroy. Government was not enlightened and the Sicilians in particular resented their subjection. Naples was not particularly industrial; the city was a 'grotesque parasite' (Hearder, 1983) living on the back of an overworked, poor peasantry. The land was owned by absentee nobles and the Church; internal customs and poor communications hindered trade. There were few entrepreneurs (0.07 per cent of the population!) but quite a few lawyers. Cereals and olive oil were the main produce and these were badly affected by the fall in prices during the first half of the nineteenth century. The kingdom was probably the least prosperous of all the Italian states, though recent research has suggested that what little industry it had was successful, and that some agricultural estates were quite productive. However, Sicilian separatism and peasant dissatisfaction rendered the kingdom potentially unstable.

Unrest in the Restoration states

At this point textbooks would normally talk about the reactionary and repressive nature of all the restored states. However, as some of the profiles of the states have suggested, recent research has called this stereotype into question. It is true that the restored governments could be *reactionary* and repressive, but this was neither the case throughout Italy nor all the time. Reaction was confined to specific rulers at specific times – most notably to Victor Emmanuel of Piedmont and Duke Francis of Modena in the immediate Restoration period, and to Papal rule between 1823 and 1846. However, these attempts at reaction led to political instability and were in fact counter-productive. For much of the time there was some modernisation, some progress, but a major failing of the restored governments was their inability to win enough support among the elite – there was insufficient distribution of patronage (jobs, pensions, titles, etc.); and of course there was also regional dissatisfaction within states, for example Sicily within Naples, and the Legations within the Papal States. But if there was disaffection, it is also true to say that the various states were not about to collapse.

KEY TERM

Reactionary – (person or regime) opposed to progress and reform.

Although the great mass of Italians remained dormant and submissive, a minority was concerned about Italy's plight. At the forefront were the *Carbonari*, or charcoal-burners, a secret society which arose in southern Italy and called for unity of organisation and purpose against Austria. In both Naples and Piedmont its members penetrated the military, finding favour among young army officers in particular. They played a key role in the so-called **Revolutions of 1820–1**. Encouraged by the successful army revolt in Spain, the Neapolitan army forced King Ferdinand to grant a constitution, and emissaries were despatched to Piedmont to incite revolution there. In Sicily a short-lived separatist revolt broke out in Palermo. However, Prince Metternich of Austria was not prepared to accept these changes and made them an international issue when the Great Powers met in congress at Troppau in 1820 and Laibach in 1821. Once he received a request for assistance from Ferdinand in 1821, he sent an army which soon overwhelmed the Neapolitan forces. Austrian troops remained until 1827. At the same time anti-Austrian sentiment flared up in Piedmont and the army called for a constitution and war against Austria. Victor Emmanuel abdicated in favour of Charles Felix, a constitution was granted, but again Austrian troops, requested by Charles Felix, soon overcame the constitutionalist forces and remained until 1823.

The second wave of unrest came in the so-called **Revolutions of 1831**, inspired by the success of the July Revolution in Paris in 1830. This time revolt broke out in Modena and spread to Parma and the northern area of the Papal States. The rulers of Modena and Parma were driven out but Lombardy and Tuscany proved impervious to the revolutionary fervour. The new Pope, Gregory XVI, appealed for

Austrian support, and very quickly Modena was occupied and Bologna pacified (though Austrian troops had to return the following year, 1832, to quell new disturbances). The French occupied Ancona (to curb the Austrians as much as to protect the Pope) and this dual foreign occupation of the Papal States continued until 1838. The old rulers were thus restored and the revolutionary fires, rapidly sparked, were just as rapidly extinguished.

Were these events really of any importance? The answer is 'yes', if we subscribe to the concept of the *Risorgimento*, because the revolutions of 1820–1 and 1831 were considered to be stepping stones on the road to unification. However, if we look at them closely this interpretation is not viable. These were not mass nationalist uprisings designed to create a unified Italy – they were in fact small-scale revolts with limited (constitutional) objectives in only a few of the states. They were confined to a few members of the elite – army officers, students, middle-class **liberals**, etc. Indeed, Garibaldi in his memoirs stated that of those who attempted to force a constitution on Victor Emmanuel in 1821, there were 'in all … six superior officers, thirty secondary officers, five physicians, ten lawyers and one Prince'. Hardly the stuff of mass revolution. Moreover, there was no coordination between revolts and no attempt to raise the masses.

Were these events of no importance at all then? To suggest this would be going too far, because they did demonstrate dissatisfaction with the Restoration governments and dislike of Austrian domination among the upper echelons of society, and both of these factors were prerequisites for what followed. However, the main lesson that emerges from these events is that Austria had a tight control over the peninsula and Prince Metternich was always prepared to use force if the existing order was challenged in any way. The people of Italy did not control their own destiny.

KEY TERM

Liberals – Liberalism was a political philosophy based on the belief in progress, the essential goodness of man and the autonomy of the individual, and standing for the protection of political and civil liberties – in this context, the desire for a constitution, representative government, freedom of speech, freedom of association and freedom of the press. This was the political philosophy of the middle classes.

Profile PRINCE METTERNICH 1773–1859

Born in Koblenz on the Rhine the son of an Austrian diplomat, he became Austrian Foreign Minister in 1809, Chancellor in 1812 and a prince in 1813. He played a prominent role in the Congress of Vienna, rearranging the German Confederation and establishing Austria's interests in Italy. He was the architect of the so-called 'Metternich System', whereby a balance of power was maintained in Europe to ensure peace. From 1815 he was the most active representative of reaction, persistently striving to stifle all change and to repress all popular and constitutional aspirations until he was brought down by the 1848 Revolutions.

Mazzini and nationalist writings

Out of a sense of frustration at the failure of these episodes, a young lawyer, Giuseppe Mazzini, in exile in Marseille founded a movement called 'Young Italy' (*Giovane Italia*) in October 1831 (see also the Picture Gallery on page 9 and the Profile on page 81). Its aim was to inspire Italians to create a unified republic by popular insurrection. Young Italy spread throughout the peninsula, replacing the *Carbonari* as the major organisation of opposition to Austria. In 1833 the movement's plans to penetrate the Sardinian army were uncovered; the following year an attempt to invade Savoy ended in dismal failure. This set the pattern for further failures in Naples in 1837, 1841 and 1844, and in the Papal States in 1837 and 1845. However, these insurrections kept the movement in the public eye and prompted Metternich to describe Mazzini as the most dangerous man in Europe. He was wrong of course, but it was a measure of the publicity Mazzini had been able to generate. Although Mazzini went on to greater fame as the leader of the ill-fated Roman Republic (see page 35), his most significant contribution to the unification of Italy was probably the influence he had on Giuseppe Garibaldi (see Chapter 4).

Mazzini's movement was a failure. Most Italians were neither nationalists nor revolutionaries – indeed, they showed remarkable loyalty to the Church, their state and their local dynasty. And yet despite the absence of nationalism in Italy, there was a remarkable outpouring of nationalist writing at this time. The views of two of these writers did have some impact. However, the effect of other creative writers such as the poet Foscolo and the novelist Manzoni, as well as the operas of Verdi and even scientific congresses, on the development of Italian identity and anti-Austrian sentiment, although probably just as significant, is difficult to measure.

In 1843 Vincenzo Gioberti published *Del primato morale e civile degli italiani* (On the Moral and Civil Primacy of the Italians), in which he called for the creation of an Italian confederation under the leadership of the Papacy, with the military cooperation of Piedmont – the holy city and the warrior province, as he put it. Gioberti rejected Mazzinian radicalism and sought to reconcile Catholicism and political liberalism. This made the Italian cause respectable. The book and its programme gained wide approval (among those who were literate – 5,000 copies were printed). But Cesare Balbo, in his book *Delle speranze d'Italia* (On the Hopes of Italy) published in 1844, felt that as Piedmont rather than the Papacy had to play the leading role in driving the Austrians out, the leadership of the federation should rest in Turin rather than Rome. Both writers rejected popular revolution for political and practical reasons: they did not want democracy and they realised that the ordinary mass of people did not have nationalist aspirations. Thus moderates placed their hopes in Piedmont and the Pope rather than the people. Charles Albert's reform programme after 1837 looked promising to many, as indeed did the election of Pius IX in 1846. The resolution of these two competing ideas would occur two years later.

Conclusion

So it would appear that Metternich was right in the statement he made in 1847: Italy was simply a geographical expression. It was not a single people. Nationalism was confined to a small minority of educated people – it never attracted the masses who formed the vast majority of the population. Even in the cities, support was very limited among the artisan class and virtually non-existent among the labouring poor. Moreover, an awareness of national self-identity among the few did not necessarily translate into a desire for unification: most Italians recognised that Italy was a diverse country, and in any event the existence of the Papacy in central Italy, with all the international implications that went with it, seemed an insuperable obstacle.

◢ Source

It would not be an exaggeration to define the early stages of Italian nationalism as an elitist phenomenon confined to urban centres where the intelligentsia congregated around institutions of learning and high culture such as literary societies, the opera and the theatre.

Michael Broers, 'Making Italy 1796–1861', in **Modern History Review**, November 1995

Why was this? We have to go back to Napoleon again. A significant number of educated Italians were deeply impressed by the efficiency of French rule. The Italian masses, on the other hand, associated it with high taxes, mass conscription and an assault on Roman Catholicism. Accordingly, the masses were alienated from the very politics the intelligentsia embraced. Furthermore, it should be remembered that the return of the old order was generally welcomed in 1814–15. The restored governments had popular support. They were seen as paternalistic, deeply Catholic and, above all, pacific. Inefficiency, lack of interference, lower taxation and no conscription were all valued by the masses.

Cavour summed up the situation when he wrote in 1846, 'In Italy a democratic revolution has no chance of success ... the masses ... are in general strongly attached to the old institutions of the country.' Thus there was no meeting of minds between the urban elite and the rural masses, and indeed no attempt was made by nationalists to court the peasantry. In contrast to rural satisfaction with the restored regimes, the urban middle classes were increasingly dissatisfied with their inefficiency, with the growth of crime and with the lack of political representation. Only in Lombardy-Venetia, where there was heavy taxation and conscription, was there genuine, widespread resentment of foreign rule – but still this did not translate into nationalism. The people of Venetia, for instance, wanted a restoration of the Republic of St Mark, not a united Italy. All this goes a long way towards explaining why unification did not come about as a result of popular insurrection, and why more Italians died fighting to prevent unification than in bringing it about. Mazzini's dream of a popular uprising was just that – a dream; and Mazzini himself had little in common with (and made little attempt to make contact with) the ordinary people.

Documentary sources

The format

Documentary sources at AS and A level tend to be contemporary sources, although some boards also use extracts from present-day historians. The object of the exercise is usually to test **recall**, **comprehension**, **comparison** and **evaluation**.

Thus an initial question might simply use the source as a prompt to test **recall** (i.e. memory/knowledge) by, for instance, referring to an historical figure in the source and asking his position in government. A second question might ask you to describe what a source is saying (i.e. **comprehension**) by expressing its content in a succinct and simplified way. It might require you to **evaluate** its usefulness. This would require you to analyse the content and possibly to determine whether or not It Is reliable – though even unreliable sources can be useful if you are aware of their unreliability, for example propaganda may give a false message but at least it tells you what false message someone is trying to get across. However, do not fall into the trap of giving a stock answer, i.e. *'but this document might be biased ...'* when you do not really know whether or not it is. You might be missing the point: many documents used in these exercises are reliable and you can take them at face value. The art of doing well is knowing what you can and cannot trust.

Yet another question might require you to **compare** sources to determine which are more useful, or how it might be possible to reconcile or explain seemingly contradictory statements. Again, an evaluation of the content is necessary and an assessment of reliability is sometimes (but not always) necessary – as indeed is your knowledge of the topic. Sometimes it is appropriate to use your own knowledge to put a source in context or refer to another document. A final question usually asks a general question which you have to answer by referring to all the sources (and you should always do this by referring to all the sources *by letter or number throughout*) and by employing your own knowledge. Of course documentary exercises vary considerably both in terms of the number and types of sources and in terms of the questions asked, but recall, comprehension, comparison and evaluation will probably be common to them all.

An exercise

Read the extracts below concerning the role of ideas in the unification of Italy, and answer all the questions which follow.

◢ Document A

The 14th of July is the feast-day of Mondo, and it is because it was the signal for the deliverance of the human race that the Order celebrates its memory. Our institution belongs to the whole world, and if its feast-day and some of its symbols derive from the French Revolution it is because France uttered the first cries of Universal Liberty and the first vigorous protests against the usurpations of Nobles, Priests and Kings. Such a great example was not ignored by Europe. From the first revolutionary outbreaks spirits revived in England, Ireland, Holland, Belgium and Italy. But the courage which destroys was not accompanied by the wisdom which rebuilds, and from all the changes to which the 14th of July was the happy prelude there remains to us only a sad lesson: that political revolutions are useful to nations only in so far as they are undertaken with popular views and are directed towards the freedom and well being of all.

From the 'notebook' of a section in Felippo Buonarroti's organisation,
Mondo *(the late 1820s)*

◢ Document B

We are a brotherhood of Italians who believe that Italy is destined to become one nation. We are republican and unitarian. Republican because theoretically every nation is destined, by the law of God and humanity, to form a free and equal community of brothers. Unitarian because federation by reducing Italy to the political impotence of Switzerland would necessarily place her under the influence of one of the neighbouring nations. The means by which we propose to reach our aims are education and insurrection by means of guerrilla bands which is the true method of warfare for all nations desirous of emancipating themselves from a foreign yoke.

From **General Instructions for the Members of Young Italy**
by Giuseppe Mazzini, 1831

◢ Document C

I intend to prove that mainly because of religion Italy possesses within herself all the necessary conditions for her national and political rebirth and that to achieve this in practice she has no need of internal revolutions nor of foreign invasions. That the Pope is naturally the civil head of Italy is a truth forecast in the nature of things. The benefits

Italy would gain from a political confederation under the moderating authority of the Pope are beyond enumeration for such an association would increase the strength of the various Princes without damaging their independence. It would remove the causes of disruptive wars and revolution at home. It would eliminate the differences in weights, measures, currencies, customs dues, speech and systems of commercial and civil administration, which so wretchedly and meanly divide the various provinces.

From **On the Moral and Civil Primacy of the Italians**
by Vincenzo Gioberti, 1843

1 Why, according to Document A, was 14 July the feast-day of *Mondo* and what lesson did the writer draw from it?   *4 marks*

2 Explain the references in Document C to 'internal revolutions' and 'foreign invasions'.   *6 marks*

3 How and why do the authors of Documents B and C differ in their approach to Italian unification?   *7 marks*

4 How far do the Documents A, B, and C explain why the attempts to unify Italy failed in the period 1815–48?   *8 marks*

OCR (formerly Oxford Delegacy), 1991

CHAPTER TWO

WHY DID ITALY FAIL TO 'MAKE HERSELF BY HERSELF' IN 1848–9?

Objectives
◢ To explore the reasons for the risings of 1848
◢ To consider why the attempt to achieve Italian independence failed
◢ To study the consequences of the failure and the lessons that needed to be learnt.

Summary introduction

The 1848 Revolutions were a Europe-wide phenomenon brought about by poor harvests, high prices and food shortages. However, on to these economic and social grievances were welded the political aspirations of the *bourgeoisie*. In Italy political changes had begun before 1848, with the election of Pius IX in 1846. Soon a wave of expectation swept the peninsula and reforms were passed everywhere except in the Kingdom of Naples. In January 1848 Palermo rose in revolt demanding autonomy for Sicily. However, far more dramatic were the events elsewhere: in February 1848 a republic was proclaimed in France, and in March rebellions broke out in Austria leading to the fall of Prince Metternich. Here was Italy's opportunity to throw off the Austrian yoke; here was an opportunity for Italian independence (though not, it should be stressed, unification). It is in this context that Charles Albert, the King of Piedmont, uttered the famous words '*L'Italia farà da sé*', literally, 'Italy will make herself by herself'. But he was wrong. The initial success of the revolutionaries had been largely artificial, brought about by the paralysis of the Restoration governments. Their fear of revolution temporarily made the rulers lose their nerve: once they regained it the revolutions were doomed. Indeed, the outcome was so disastrous that in Italian '*fare un quarantotto*' (making a '48) became a popular phrase to describe chaos and confusion. Before we decide what went wrong, we should take a look at what actually happened.

The events in detail

Although the economic background to events in Italy in 1848 was important – poor harvests, high prices and continuing high taxes at a time of hardship compounded unrest – the Italian revolutions were more political than economic. As we have indicated, the story begins earlier in 1846. In June of that year, Giovanni Maria Mastai-Ferretti was elected as Pope Pius IX. The election of this little-known man was a compromise to avoid either a too liberal or too conservative candidate. His election came as a surprise but he went on to be the longest serving Pope (so far). His affability provoked a positive response among the citizens of Rome, and when he immediately issued a general amnesty for political prisoners he was hailed as a liberal saviour. Moreover, the jubilation took on a decidedly anti-Austrian tone which Pius did nothing to curb.

The Pope went on to plan reforms and in 1847 he relaxed press censorship, formed a civic guard and established an indirectly elected advisory body, the *Consulta*. The cry *'Viva Pio Nono'* went up all over Italy. All of this suggested he was the figure heralded by Gioberti to liberate Italy, but this was to misread him completely. Pius IX was not a liberal and had no intention of freeing Italy from Austria – rather, he was a man who believed in gradual change in order to prevent revolution. He himself stated that reform was a manifestation of his benevolence; he did not subscribe to any theory of the rights of man. But there was an inherent contradiction in his position, and even in 1847 popular pressure pushed him further than he wanted to go. Soon events would overtake him completely. Thus his pontificate had increased expectations and raised the political temperature.

His election was greeted positively by the King of Piedmont. Charles Albert was also a misunderstood figure. Like Pius, he was not a liberal, but he increasingly adopted an anti-Austrian stance and came to believe he would liberate Italy from the Austrian yoke. Thus, here too was an ambiguity: embracing a liberal cause outside Piedmont, yet holding on to autocracy within it.

Profile CHARLES ALBERT (CARLO ALBERTO) 1789–1849

Charles Albert was briefly appointed regent during the rising of 1821, but was exiled by the new king, Charles Felix. Appointed viceroy in Sardinia in 1829, he succeeded to the throne when Charles Felix died in 1831. Having lost the liberal friends of his youth, he had become 'a solitary figure with a cadaverous face, a long, ungainly figure, and awkward manners' (Hearder, 1983). Although he introduced a number of liberal reforms to modernise Piedmont, he was opposed to a constitution which he saw as a step on the road to republicanism. Nevertheless, he was forced to grant one in 1848. However, his failure in 1848–9 led to his abdication. He retired to Portugal and died there three months later.

The rise in tension in 1847 persuaded Field Marshal Radetzky, the 81-year-old Austrian commander in Italy, to reinforce his garrison in Ferrara in the Papal States in July. The Pope was not happy with this development and patriots everywhere applauded his opposition. Austrian policy had the effect of pushing the Papal States and Piedmont together. The Pope went on to propose a tariff league which Tuscany promptly joined. However, Charles Albert's hesitation earned him the epithet, 'the wobbling king'. Finally, in November 1848, a Customs League Treaty was signed between the Papacy, Piedmont and Tuscany and there was much talk of a political league to follow. This projected Italian political league was supported in December 1847 by a new newspaper, *Il Risorgimento*, founded by Camillo di Cavour and Cesare Balbo (among others).

This then was the background to 1848. There was much tension, rising anti-Austrian feeling and talk of Italian independence.

Chronological chart

	Piedmont	Lombardy	Venetia	Central Duchies	Papacy	Naples/ Sicily
1848 Jan		Riots in Milan				Revolution in Palermo. Ferdinand issues Constitution
Feb	Charles Albert grants Constitution			Grand Duke of Tuscany grants Constitution		
Mar	Charles Albert declares war on Austria	Austrians driven out of Milan	Revolt in Venice	Rulers of Modena and Parma flee	Pope grants Constitution	
Apr					Pope condemns war against Austria	Sicily declares independence. Restoration of royal authority in Naples
May June July	Charles Albert defeated at Custoza					
Aug	Armistice with Austria	Austrians reconquer Lombardy				
Sep Oct Nov Dec					Pope flees	
1849 Jan				Grand Duke of Tuscany flees		
Feb					Proclamation of Roman Republic	

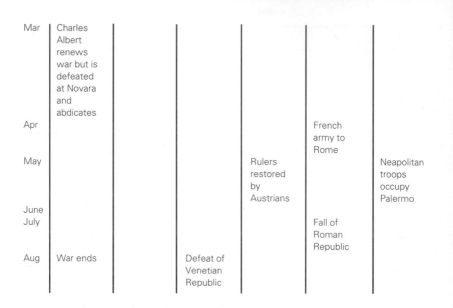

Mar	Charles Albert renews war but is defeated at Novara and abdicates				
Apr				French army to Rome	
May			Rulers restored by Austrians		Neapolitan troops occupy Palermo
June					
July				Fall of Roman Republic	
Aug	War ends		Defeat of Venetian Republic		

The year 1848 opened with unrest in Milan where, as a protest against harsh Austrian rule, the citizens stopped smoking (tobacco was an Austrian state monopoly worth in excess of four million lira a year in tax). More significant was the uprising in Palermo which soon spread to the whole of Sicily and forced King Ferdinand II to grant a constitution for both Naples and Sicily on 29 January.

Profile FERDINAND II 1810–59

Ferdinand became King of the Two Sicilies in 1830. He was 'an ignorant man, who never read a book, could not spell, and despised intellectuals. One of his main pleasures consisted in playing childish pranks on his courtiers' (Hearder, 1983). Initially his rule was promising, but after the death of his first wife in 1836 he married a Habsburg and gave himself up to Austrian counsel. He became increasingly conservative. He survived the revolutions of 1848–9, and his heavy bombardment of Sicily during its recovery earned him the name 'King Bomba'. His rule became increasingly harsh – his reign was described by Gladstone as 'the negation of God erected into a system of government' – and the unpopularity of his regime directly contributed to its rapid collapse after his death.

After a month of pressure, Charles Albert too finally granted Piedmont a constitution, the *Statuto* (see page 38), on 8 February. Three days later Leopold, Grand Duke of Tuscany, followed suit. At this point the European political landscape dramatically transformed. On 24 February a revolution in Paris removed Louis Philippe, the last King of France, but more significant for the states of Italy was Metternich's fall from power in Vienna on 13 March. This precipitated full-scale uprisings in both Venice and Milan. The Italian rulers were by now being overtaken by events.

After a glorious 'five days' (*cinque giornate* – 18–22 March) of heroic fighting by the populace of Milan, Radetzky was forced to withdraw his garrison. In Venice, where the Austrian garrison consisted of mainly Italian troops, a peaceful mutiny signalled the collapse of Austrian power. The rulers of Parma and Modena fled. Although Daniel Manin declared a republic in Venice, the Milanese, after some debate, looked to Piedmont for help. Once again Charles Albert hesitated, but then on 23 March Piedmontese troops moved into Lombardy, thereby declaring war on Austria. The King promised to support the aspiration of independence (there was no talk of unification) and famously declared that Italy will do it alone – *L'Italia farà da sé* – though this had not a little to do with his fear of intervention by the French Republic (which might lead to his overthrow). Popular pressure ensured that Ferdinand of Naples and Leopold of Tuscany also pledged their support to the crusade for independence. However, the truth is that Charles Albert was more concerned to extend Piedmontese dominion than to embrace any federal political solution, and the other princes suspected as much.

The 'Italian cause' was further undermined by the Pope's reluctance to declare war on Catholic Austria. His hand was forced by his own commander-in-chief, General Durando, who hijacked the Papal forces. On 29 April, in an 'allocution', the Pope finally made his position public, revealing that he could not join the crusade against Austria. Reaction was immediate and negative. Many believed he had dealt a fatal blow to the Italian cause. Yet Italian success continued, aided more by Austrian paralysis than Piedmontese prowess. The Piedmontese advance had been painfully slow and no attempt had been made to attack Radetzky (who withdrew into the Quadrilateral –

four forts on the Lombard-Venetian border: Peschiera, Verona, Legnago and Mantua; see Figure 3 on page 60) or cut off his lines of communication. Indeed, Charles Albert was more concerned with annexation than military victory – collecting votes while Radetzky collected men, as the Milanese politician Cattaneo pointedly put it. Political developments looked promising but proved premature. In May Parma and Modena voted to join with Piedmont, as did Lombardy in June and Venice in July. Charles Albert may have defeated the republicans in these states but he had not defeated the one man he needed to. Radetzky was both undefeated and resolute. He ignored Vienna's decision to make concessions and give up Lombardy and once reinforced, he struck at Custoza on 25 July, broke the Piedmontese war effort and reoccupied Lombardy in August.

Charles Albert now asked for French help, only to be informed that an earlier request might have been successful! Fortunately for Piedmont, Austrian fear of French intervention led to an armistice in August. The sudden collapse of the Piedmontese war effort came as a shock, and criticism of both the Pope and Charles Albert was widespread. The King determined to renew the war at the earliest opportunity. Meanwhile in Rome the situation was degenerating. In November the Pope's first minister was assassinated, Rome slipped into chaos and the Pope fled across the border to Gaeta in the Kingdom of Naples. When a republic was declared in Rome in February 1849, Pius IX appealed to Austria for restoration. This offended patriots and set the Pope against the Italian cause. It also proved to be problematic in Turin where the King of Piedmont was planning to resume the war with the Austrians with Roman backing (and in the erroneous belief that he had French backing too).

On 12 March 1849, Charles Albert denounced the armistice, but before the Piedmontese soldiers could advance one metre Field Marshal Radetzky, who had anticipated this development, took the offensive and smashed them at the battle of Novara on 23 March. The war was over before it had begun. The next day Charles Albert abdicated in favour of his son, Victor Emmanuel, who met with Radetzky and obtained a reasonable armistice. In what proved to be significant for the future, the Austrians insisted that Piedmont keep its constitution in the belief that only in this way could the monarchy be saved.

The Austrians then went on to restore the Grand Duke of Tuscany and the rulers of Parma and Modena in May. In the same month Ferdinand recovered control of Sicily. Italian hopes now rested with the republics of Rome and Venice, but at this point France and Austria came together to restore the Pope. The Austrians occupied the Legations while France landed troops at Civitavecchia, not far from Rome, in April. Despite the enlightened leadership of Mazzini and the valour of General Garibaldi, the Roman Republic finally fell at the beginning of July. Then in August Venice, worn down by bombardment (some of which was aerial, from balloons) and hunger, and plagued by cholera, finally capitulated. The quest for Italian independence was over – for a decade. In 1850 the Pope returned to Rome and the Piedmontese Chamber approved the peace treaty with Austria. Reaction had triumphed.

Analysis

So why had Italy failed to 'make herself by herself'?

First of all, there were too many divisions among the princes, the politicians and the people, divisions over aims, purpose and outcome. Ferdinand of Naples had been pushed into an anti-Austrian stance against his will by popular pressure. The Pope, too, had been swept along by others' aspirations until his position became untenable. These two soon threw in their lot with the Austrians. Charles Albert had his own agenda – to stop revolutionary republicanism and to promote Piedmontese aggrandisement, though even the gondoliers of Venice expressed their doubts about this development when they sang 'fusion is really confusion'! The leaders of the revolt in Milan were divided between moderates and republicans, as were the leaders of Venice. Many mistrusted Piedmont, as they did the Roman Republic when it later invited union; the governments of Tuscany, Venice and Sicily all refused. Indeed, the latter was only really interested in separatism and independence. In addition, after Custoza governments came and went with alarming rapidity. There was no political stability, no political continuity. Constitutionalism brought chaos. Men of property everywhere feared social revolution and this factor also prevented unanimity of action. Hatred of the Austrians only went so far and was insufficient to reconcile the variety of political aspirations. If their support for a free Italy unified the rebels, politics clearly divided them.

Secondly, Italy's window of opportunity was open only as long as Austrian paralysis lasted. In any event, paralysis in Vienna was countered by the resolution of Radetzky in Verona. This remarkable elderly man was the key to Austrian success. Whereas Vienna was prepared to make a deal with Charles Albert, Radetzky was confident he could be victorious – and so he should have been; he had the numbers (particularly after he was reinforced in the summer). Although over one-third of his 70,000 strong army consisted of unreliable Italians (and quite a few unreliable Hungarians as well), he still outnumbered the Piedmontese who could only raise about 20–30,000 at the most. As in previous upheavals, it was the strength of the Austrian army that proved decisive, as was the strength of the French army in overcoming the Roman Republic.

Profile RADETZKY, COUNT JOHANN JOSEPH 1766–1858

An Austrian soldier born in Bohemia, Radetzky fought against the Turks in the 1780s and against the French during the Revolutionary and Napoleonic wars. After temporary retirement in 1829, he was appointed Commander-in-Chief of Lombardy from 1831 and promoted to Field Marshal in 1836. He fathered an illegitimate child at the age of 79 and decisively defeated the Piedmontese in 1848–9, by which time he was an octogenarian. He ruled Lombardy-Venetia with an iron hand until he was retired in 1857 aged 90. During his lifetime he was wounded seven times and had nine horses shot from underneath him! The elder Strauss wrote a march in his honour.

Thirdly, in contrast to Radetzky, Charles Albert was inadequate to the task, an incompetent general and a poor leader. His entire premise that the Piedmontese army alone could take on the Austrians and win was wrong. The army itself lacked numbers, equipment and competent officers, and did not even have maps of Lombardy! Moreover, Charles Albert appeared to be more concerned to defeat the republicans of Milan and Venice than the Austrians, and would not use volunteer troops whom he considered to be unreliable radicals. In addition, he wrongly feared a French invasion and left much of his army guarding the western border. Perversely, in 1849 he wrongly assumed that the new French President, Louis Napoleon, would actually come to his aid, though no agreement had ever been reached. The truth is Charles Albert was more concerned about extending Piedmont and preserving his own autocratic power than anything else. He was not the right man to lead the movement for Italian independence.

Lastly, it should be pointed out that, except in Lombardy and Venetia where direct Austrian rule was resented, most Italians were oblivious to what was going on.

◢ Source

The protagonists of this politically muddled, militarily disastrous and economically counter-productive display of idealism and heroism were the small elite of revolutionary romantic intellectuals which had been formed in the great debate of the previous years ... Popular involvement, though genuine enough where it occurred, was confined to the conscripts sent by Piedmont and the other Italian states and the populace of cities under siege. It scarcely touched the mass of peasants, although some of them helped the fleeing remnants of what they always called the 'rebels' to survive, nor was it promoted by the small emergent class of entrepreneurs, although many of them certainly hoped to gain by any success of the movement.

Roger Ahsalom, **Italy since 1800** (Longman, 1995)

Consequences and conclusion

Because of the military superiority of the Austrians, the revolutions had been an almost total failure, though it should be remembered that they failed everywhere in Germany and in the other Habsburg lands as well. A reaction set in and harsh autocratic government returned – the 'Second Restoration' was considerably more repressive than the first, though in truth the regimes were not that strong and in many cases had to be propped up by the Austrians. The government of Naples was particularly harsh – in Sicily the hated *macinato* (grain tax – see page 91) was reintroduced and raised. In the Papal States the Pope was maintained by permanent garrisons of foreign troops, the French in Rome and the Austrians in the Legations. Austrian troops also remained in Tuscany, Modena and Parma. Lombardy and Venetia were more firmly under Austrian control than ever before and the land tax was raised by a massive 30 per cent. Radetzky's rule was oppressive. The cause of Italian independence had been set back and contemporaries could have been forgiven for thinking that it had been permanently extinguished.

However, a number of important lessons were to be learnt from the failures of 1848–9.

1 It was quite clear that Italy could not make 'herself by herself'. Her forces were no match for Austria and she clearly needed outside help. Accordingly, Piedmont had to be strengthened, retain the leadership of 'Italy' and be an attractive ally for a major power opposed to Austria (i.e. France).

2 The Papacy was no longer a vehicle for Italian patriotism, and anti-clericalism became very much part of the cause for independence. However, the real lesson was that it was best to leave the Pope alone. The Papacy was still internationally important and the fate of the pontiff was still the concern of other Catholic powers.

3 Piedmont now offered an alternative to the princes and Mazzinian republicanism. When the 'revolution of the princes' had failed, Mazzini had announced that the 'revolution of the people' would now succeed, but in fact neither had been viable (the vast majority of Italians had not been particularly insurrectionary in 1848–9). What Piedmont now offered was the constitutional way. The survival of the constitution – the **Statuto** – proved to be significant. It was attractive to the middle classes of central and northern Italy as well as to many members of the aristocratic elite elsewhere, who realised that without Austrian support their governments offered them little real protection.

KEY TERM

The **Statuto** – The importance of the Piedmontese constitution that Charles Albert conceded on 8 February 1848 was not only that it survived the upheavals of 1848–9, but that it became the basis for Italy's constitution in the 1860s and lasted (with changes) until 1947. It allowed for the existence of two Chambers, the upper nominated by the King, the lower elected. Both Chambers and the King had the right to introduce legislation. Also granted were freedom of association and equal rights to citizenship and public office. A later electoral law restricted the franchise to about 2 per cent of the population (87,000 initially). This was very narrow but comparable to Britain at the time. The Lower Chamber established the right to examine and vote on the budget annually. The monarchy retained considerable power but was weak after 1848–9, and this enabled constitutional government to develop (though party politics did not).

Indeed, Piedmont proved something of a magnet for patriots from all over Italy and although figures are hard to come by, at least 20,000, and possibly as many as 100,000, settled there in the following decade. Turin became the centre of Italian political culture. Piedmont's relative independence of Habsburg authority and the very fact that it had a (albeit limited) political life – via both the constitution and a relatively free press – made it unique and gave hope for the future. And the dream did live on. One of the other important legacies of 1848–9, which was later used to buttress the myth of the *Risorgimento*, were stories of that heroic time, in particular the exploits of Garibaldi in Rome. Not only had he driven a Neapolitan army back across the border and been wounded in the process, but he also managed to hold off a French force of 20,000 – over three times as large as his own – for almost a month. But while Mazzini escaped in disguise, Garibaldi called upon his soldiers to continue the fight: 'I offer neither pay nor quarters nor provisions. I offer hunger, thirst, forced marches, battle and death. Let him who loves his country in his heart and not with his lips only, follow me.' Thereafter he fought on in the mountains with 4,000 volunteers until forced to flee to the neutral territory of San Marino, a harrowing journey which led to the death of his pregnant wife.

At this point books on this subject go on to focus on Piedmont and its Prime Minister from 1852, Cavour – and this book is no exception. However, we must be careful not to read history backwards. Italian independence, let alone unification, looked most unlikely in the 1850s, and we should remember that the Hungarians, Slavs and Poles all had to await the cataclysmic First World War and the year 1919 before their dreams were realised. In Italy's case a much smaller war – the Crimean War – was to prove of some significance (see page 47).

Essay writing

A few tips

The purpose of the essay question is to show that you have mastered the material on a particular topic and are able to support or refute arguments – your own as well as those of the historians you have read.

You must above all **address the question**, which can mean simply clarifying its meaning by defining key terms if there are ambiguities, or answering the question straight away if there are not.

The greatest enemy of the effective essay is **irrelevance**. Anything which interrupts the flow of your argument must be left out (remember you have limited time). However, facts and examples which are related to your argument are as important as the argument itself; those which are not related are totally valueless. Do not think that if you simply put every detail down, they will make your case for you. They will not. This narrative approach will only achieve a low grade at best. You must learn to be analytical and refer to the question whenever it is appropriate. It cannot be emphasised too strongly that most AS and A level casualties in history are those students who have not mastered **relevance**.

As far as **style** is concerned, you should maintain the pressure of persuasion on the examiner by using short and concise sentences. Remember ABC – Accuracy, Brevity and Clarity – are the most important characteristics of style.

A suggested format

You should use the **introduction** to address the question, define its terms and in effect answer it by explaining your view. You should remember that examiners are marking hundreds of AS and A level essays in a very short period of time and they want to know if you know the answer (there can be several 'right' ones but many more 'wrong' ones). They do not want to have to wade through pages of narrative until the question is finally addressed in the conclusion (*'thus in answer to the question, we can see that …'*). You have to get the examiner on your side right from the start.

If you adopt this approach, the rest of the essay will then justify the position you have taken at the beginning by developing the argument with factual support. By the time you reach the end, your **conclusion** should be almost superfluous; you have answered the question and you should have the marks in the bag. You might wish to reiterate your argument or further impress the examiner by pointing forward or looking back, outside the confines of the question, in order to show the breadth of your knowledge.

Some actual essays:

1 Explain the failure of Italy to achieve national unification in the first half of the nineteenth century.
2 Why did Italy fail to achieve independence in 1848–9?
3 Why did the Italians fail in 1848–9 and succeed in 1859–61?
4 What were the lessons of 1848–9 for Italian nationalists and how did Cavour show he had learnt those lessons?

The first essay is broad in scope, but you could begin by questioning the question. After all, national unification was not achieved because no one attempted it! But then you still need to discuss the obstacles to unification – the political geography of the peninsula, Austrian dominance, the absence of nationalism, the impracticality of the plans proposed by Mazzini and Gioberti and others, etc. In addition to 1848 you also need to discuss 1820 and 1831, to show that these events did not have unification as their purpose either.

The second essay is much more specific and requires you to focus on 1848–9, much as this chapter has done. In the third essay a discussion of 1848–9 would only take up a third or a half of the essay at most as you are required to concentrate on what came later. Similarly, in the last question the bulk of your focus is on what Cavour did, though you clearly have to identify the lessons of 1848–9. You are more likely to be set a question on the later events, but you cannot afford to be unaware of the events of 1848–9.

Documentary exercise

Read the extracts on 1848 below and then answer all the questions which follow.

◢ Document A

We, out of love for our common race, understanding, as we do, what is now happening, and supported by public opinion, hasten to associate ourselves with the unanimous admiration which Italy bestows on you.

Peoples of Lombardy and Venetia, our arms which were concentrating on your frontier when you forestalled events by liberating your glorious Milan, are now coming to offer you in the latter phase of your fight the help which a brother expects from a brother, and a friend from a friend.

We support your just desires, confident as we are in the help of the God whose helpful hand has wonderfully enabled Italy to rely on her own strength (Italia farà da sé).

In order to show more openly our feelings of Italian brotherhood, we have ordered our troops as they move into Lombardy and Venice to carry the Cross of Savoy imposed on the tricolour flag of Italy.

From Charles Albert's proclamation to Lombardy and Venice, Turin, 23 March 1848

◢ Document B

Seeing that some at present desire that We too, along with the other princes of Italy and their subjects, should engage in war against the Austrians, We have thought it convenient to proclaim clearly and openly, in this our solemn assembly, that such a measure is altogether alien from our counsels.

And in this place We cannot refrain from repudiating before the face of all nations, the treacherous advice, published moreover in journals, and in various works, of those who would have the Roman Pontiff to be the head and to preside over the formation of some sort of novel republic of the whole Italian people. Rather on this occasion, moved hereto by the love We bear them, We do urgently warn and exhort the said Italian people to abstain with all diligence from the like counsels, deceitful and ruinous to Italy herself and to abide close attachments to their respective sovereigns.

From the allocution of Pius IX on 29 April 1848

◢ Document C

The subsequent story that Charles Albert had been counting the days until he could attack Austria does not square with the fact that his army was entirely unprepared for such a war. It evidently had no plans nor even any maps of Lombardy, and almost all its strength was rather posted on the French frontier as a defence against the menace of republicanism.

Four days were wasted at Turin in deciding whether or not to fight. Then with greatly superior forces, a slow, timid advance took place which did nothing at all to harry Radetzky or to seize the mountain passes and cut off his supplies. Instead of marching at once on Brescia or Verona, not until the second week in April did any serious fighting commence, and by that time the Austrians were well protected inside the Quadrilateral. Garibaldi's offer of help was turned down by the king on the grounds that to accept support from mere volunteers and ex-outlaws would be dishonourable for the army.

This fundamental military weakness was made worse by political differences. Instead of playing for support from the popular elements who had chiefly manned the barricades at Milan and other towns, Charles Albert preferred the small aristocratic element in Lombardy. Instead of concentrating on the war, he insisted on holding a plebiscite to make sure of the political fusion of Lombardy and Venice with Piedmont even though this was bound to arouse suspicions of Piedmontese aggrandisement and discourage other elements in Naples, Tuscany and Rome who wanted a new union of Italy. Politics at once became bitter, and the republicans and federalists gradually broke away from what looked to them like an essentially royalist anti-revolutionary war.

From Count Casati, **New Revelations** on the facts in regard to Milan during 1847–8
published in 1885; Casati was Mayor of Milan in 1848

1 What reasons does Casati give in Document C for the ineffectiveness of Charles Albert's invasion of Lombardy? *4 marks*

2 What was meant by *Italia farà da sé*, in Document A, and who advocated this solution to Italy's problems? *6 marks*

3 Compare Documents A and C as sources for Charles Albert's motives for invading Lombardy. *7 marks*

4 How fully do Documents A, B, and C explain the failure of the 1848 Revolutions in Italy? *8 marks*

OCR (formerly Oxford Delegacy), 1989

CHAPTER THREE

WHAT WERE CAVOUR'S AIMS AND WHAT DID HE ACHIEVE (TO APRIL 1860)?

Objectives

◢ To determine Cavour's aims and achievements

◢ To study Napoleon III's aims and explain his participation in Italian affairs

◢ To examine the outcome of the war of 1859

◢ To consider how far the goal of unification was, or was not, part of these events.

Part A: Cavour, Piedmont and the leadership of Italy, 1850–7

Background: Piedmont

Gradually and reluctantly the Piedmontese monarchy had, by the late 1830s, come to accept that its dynastic ambitions could not be sustained without better administration and economic expansion, and the latter improvements were also desired by the more progressive elements of the elite. In this way dynastic ambitions and liberal aspirations converged, though the monarchy had no wish to relinquish power. Reforms began in the late 1830s, but it was the revolutions of 1848–9 that accelerated the process. Basically it was the constitution that made peaceful reform possible, and the failure of 1848–9 showed that reform was essential. The *Statuto* (see page 38) bound the elite and the monarchy together and enabled them to undertake change without social revolution. Although not the sole architect of reform, Count Camillo di Cavour came to play the most decisive role.

Background: Cavour

Cavour came from an old (French-speaking) noble family, but became a liberal in outlook at an early age. One of his most formative experiences was his visit to England in 1835 where he believed he had glimpsed the future. He visited factories, rode on the Liverpool to Manchester railway and attended parliamentary debates. He became a firm believer in progress. Political progress meant that an increasing number of responsible citizens should have a share in power. He was opposed to autocracy (he called for a constitution in 1847) and the political power of the Church (he supported anti-clerical legislation), but he feared democracy. He believed there was a middle way. He favoured social reform but not socialism. Economic progress meant that there should be increasing material benefits for all and that this could be achieved by, among other things, free trade and railway development.

As far as 'Italy' was concerned, Cavour was aware that there was an Italian question (as distinct from solely Piedmontese concerns) and he looked upon Tuscans and Romagnans as fellow Italians, but more often than not when he referred to 'my country' he was referring to Piedmont. In 1848 Cavour speculated about a new kingdom of northern Italy, but he felt that a single federated state was something rather distant. Moreover, he did not know the south of Italy at all; indeed he did not know the rest of Italy all that well either – he was never to travel south of Florence. And he recognised that the significance to other Catholic powers of the Pope's international position would be an obstacle to unification (something Garibaldi always failed to appreciate). It should also be remembered that the nationalist ideal of unification was associated with Mazzinian revolutionary republicanism, which was another (very important) reason for rejecting it.

In 1844 Cavour had predicted that Italy could only achieve independence if there occurred a 'new settlement' among the Great Powers, or a 'great commotion'. He was aware of the limitations of a small power. His main concern was the recovery and modernisation of Piedmont after the humiliations of 1848–9: Italian unification did not feature in his thinking. He championed the creation of a progressive, well-ordered state to set an example and act as a contrast to the backwardness of the Papal States and Naples. Independent and ambitious, and not too scrupulous in his methods, Cavour only emerged as a public figure during the revolutions. He was to dominate politics thereafter.

Cavour in office – the early years

Prior to Cavour coming to office d'Azeglio, Prime Minister from April 1849, had succeeded in making the parliamentary system work. He had proposed radical changes in Church–state relations which culminated in the Siccardi Laws of 1850–1. Cavour spoke in favour of this legislation and joined d'Azeglio's cabinet in October 1850 as Minister of Agriculture, Industry and Commerce. He immediately inspired the government to sign a series of free trade agreements with Britain, France and Belgium and even Austria among others, and he introduced a general tariff reduction. Although trade trebled in ten years, *laissez-faire* was not enough: state intervention was needed as well, and the state had a responsibility to finance the army, public works and railways. Accordingly, in 1851, Cavour added the Ministry of Finance to his responsibilities and his banking skills facilitated loans for limited state intervention. In addition, he reformed the credit system and developed a central bank and other banking institutions.

As d'Azeglio's government moved to the right Cavour resigned in May 1852, only to come back as Prime Minister at the end of the year (though he had to drop the Civil Marriage Bill to please the King). He completed his fiscal programme in 1853 by abolishing all duties on imported grain. In addition, he reformed the bureaucracy, purged the magistracy and opened up the higher ranks of the army. All of these measures reduced the power of the reactionary aristocracy which had dominated these institutions hitherto. The effect of these reforms was to make Piedmont the most modern state in Italy. The weakness of the southern economy compared with that of the north became ever more apparent. Piedmont's constitutionalism, parliamentary life, religious liberty and economic progress revitalised her reputation and 'served as a beacon to the oppressed of the peninsula' (Davis, 1988). Cavour hoped her progressivism would create a European climate favourable to Turin and critical of Vienna. In particular he wished to curry favour with France and Britain. However, the reforming initiative suffered increasingly from its subordination to matters of foreign policy, to which we now turn.

Cavour and the Crimean War

According to Denis Mack Smith in his 1985 biography of Cavour, the Prime Minister inherited the basis for his foreign policy from d'Azeglio and Balbo. They had wished to free Italy from Austria and were convinced that Piedmont must at the very least acquire French or English help, or preferably both. Cavour wholeheartedly embraced this policy and made no bones about what his ultimate aim was – 'the aggrandisement of Piedmont', as he put it.

When Cavour went to Paris in 1852 prior to becoming Prime Minister, he met Louis Napoleon who spoke of his desire for an Italian federation under the honorary presidency of the Pope, but effectively directed by Piedmont. He also made similar promises to successive Piedmontese ambassadors. Napoleon's sympathy for the Italian cause was of long standing. However, in office he did nothing to promote it. Rather the reverse. He sustained the Pope with French troops and later, at the time of the Crimean War, he courted the Austrians. Napoleon was described by contemporaries as sphinx-like, a reference to the difficulty they had in determining his motives; however, Bismarck described him as a sphinx without a riddle. Bismarck was probably right: there was no mystery at all. Basically Napoleon was concerned to put French interests and that of his family before anything else, but because of his indecisive nature he tended to chop and change which made him unpredictable. He may have stated, *'Je suis résolu à faire quelque chose pour l'Italie que j'aime comme une seconde patrie'* (I am resolved to do something for Italy which I love like a second homeland) but this was just empty talk. When he proclaimed himself Emperor Napoleon III in 1852, he had to reassure the other Great Powers that the Empire meant peace and that he was not going to emulate his uncle, the great Napoleon; foreign adventures were out of the question. In any event Cavour himself could not begin to contemplate a confrontation with Austria so soon after the debacle of 1848–9. In 1853 he even went out of his way to try to warn the Austrians of a Mazzinian uprising in Milan (which was easily suppressed).

The outbreak of the Crimean War between Turkey and Russia in October 1853, followed by Britain and France's participation on Turkey's side in April 1854, transformed the situation somewhat and clearly raised the possibility of a redrawing of the map of Europe. However, the old view that Cavour took advantage of the situation to participate, thereby raising the Italian question to the forefront of Great Power diplomacy, has not survived recent research. This was not another step on the road to unification as the proponents of the *Risorgimento* would have us believe. Increasingly Cavour is shown to have been swept along by events. Piedmont was pressured by Britain and France into joining the war so as to reassure Austria. The leaders in London and Paris wanted Vienna on their side, but they had to ensure that if the Austrians participated trouble would not break out in Italy behind their backs. In addition, Britain wanted Piedmontese manpower.

Foreign policy in Piedmont was always decided with little reference to parliament and to some extent it remained part of the royal prerogative. Accordingly, the allies made every effort to court Victor Emmanuel. Headstrong and not very intelligent, the King was soon very keen to join the war, and it seems likely that Cavour persuaded the cabinet to go to war in January 1855 to save his own political skin, to forestall his dismissal and pre-empt the King. Whatever the truth, once the decision was made, Cavour became enthusiastic about the war and did see it as an opportunity to keep in with Napoleon and gain something for Piedmont.

However, the truth is that Piedmont was offered absolutely nothing in return for its participation. Already in December 1854 Napoleon III had promised Vienna that he would guarantee her Italian possessions if Austria took the western side. Quite simply, Austrian help was much more valuable to Britain and France than that of Piedmont.

Piedmont sent a small contingent to Crimea (18,000 in total) which distinguished itself in one minor battle – sufficient to boost Piedmontese prestige a little. Then in December 1855 (much to Cavour's dissatisfaction) Austria's threat to Russia brought the war to a premature end and gave the Habsburgs a place at the peace conference. During the war, Cavour told Victor Emmanuel that his objective was 'to extend the boundaries of the royal domain and ensure its precedence over the rest of Italy', but even he realised that this would not be the outcome of the peace conference, especially since Austria had not aligned with Russia.

In January 1856, Cavour sent a realistic letter to Napoleon expressing the limits of his aims at that time. All he could hope for was a softening of Habsburg rule in Lombardy-Venetia and of Bourbon rule in Naples;

he requested that Austrian troops should evacuate the Papal Legations and possibly that the territory be transferred to either Tuscany or Modena. He made no claims of territory for Piedmont.

The Congress of Paris opened on 25 February 1856 and the presidency fell to the French Foreign Minister, Count Walewski, who had no sympathy for Piedmont or the Italian cause. The Treaty of Paris was finally signed on 30 March and Cavour obtained absolutely nothing for Piedmont. Indeed, Napoleon was most unhelpful; apart from the fact that he could not consider another war so soon after the last one, his main concern appears to have been to secure the Pope as godfather to his first child. Cavour did at least manage to obtain for Piedmont equal status at the conference and there was discussion of the Italian question on 8 April; however, the only outcome was that Britain and France broke off diplomatic relations with Naples when King Ferdinand failed to reform. Moreover, Cavour's visit to England, where he intrigued with the Tory opposition, proved to be a disaster, turning a potential ally into a potential enemy. Further, on 15 April Britain and France signed a secret treaty with Austria guaranteeing the status quo, a development unknown to Cavour until he read about it in the French newspapers on 8 May! So, far from being a step on the road to a glorious settlement of the Italian question, Piedmont's participation in the Crimean War had been unpopular and unproductive. Cavour returned to Turin after two and a half months away, empty-handed and convinced of his failure, though he used all his political skill to persuade parliament otherwise.

Indeed, it was not all doom and gloom. Piedmont had been accorded equal status at the conference, the Italian question had been raised and it was clear that Cavour had established himself as spokesman for matters Italian. Piedmont's participation in the war had confirmed her status as the leading state in Italy, a factor recognised earlier in 1854 by Garibaldi's return and in 1855 by the conversion of the erstwhile republican Daniel Manin, when he called on Piedmont to unify Italy. Moreover, unbeknown to Cavour at the time, the Crimean War had transformed the international situation. In particular, Austria's ambivalent approach to the war had left her isolated. By failing to support Russia she had forfeited her friendship, and by failing to commit to military participation on behalf of Britain and France she had not earned their gratitude either. There would be a price to pay for Austria's indecision. Austria's isolation would prove to be crucial – without it, it is most unlikely that Napoleon III would have ever contemplated a war with the Habsburgs, as he was to do a few years later.

Cavour and the National Society

As we have mentioned, Daniel Manin was one of the first of the radical republicans to break with Mazzini as he came to realise that Piedmont stood more chance of expelling the Austrians than did a popular uprising; likewise Giuseppe Garibaldi. These men and others assumed the name the 'National Society' in August 1857 (though it originated in 1855–6). The credo of the new organisation subordinated the issue of eventual political structure to the more pressing need for independence, and supported Cavour and the House of Savoy so long as they worked on behalf of Italy (but not all members trusted either Cavour in particular or the Piedmontese in general). Though never more than 4,000 in number, Cavour was happy to exploit the patriots and draw as many as possible away from Mazzinian extremism. Clearly he saw the National Society as a means of taming the republicans.

In fact, Cavour had met with Manin on several occasions when he was in Paris at the beginning of 1856. Interestingly, Cavour found Manin too much preoccupied with the 'idea of Italian unity and other such nonsense', an idea he regarded as Mazzinian. Cavour remained interested in emancipation (i.e. independence), not unification. But he was playing a dangerous double game. He wanted to foment political instability in the peninsula, but at the same time he wanted to ensure that no radical revolution occurred. Thus he oscillated between encouraging activists and tipping off the conservative rulers! In particular he intrigued in the Legations, Tuscany and Modena, and it is possible that he gave Mazzini some latitude by allowing him to operate from Genoa. However, the latter's uprising in Sicily in 1856 was a failure, as were the uprisings in Genoa and Leghorn the following year. Carlo Piscane's attempt to raise a revolt in Naples (also 1857) was particularly embarrassing for Cavour as he hijacked a Piedmontese vessel, though his failure clearly demonstrated the peasants' indifference to revolutionary socialism. It was quite obvious that the Mazzinian way had no future.

Cavour returned from Paris keen to devote himself to foreign affairs. In private he talked of war with Austria within three years, but he knew Piedmont could not 'do it alone'. He also tried to play a double game with the powers, playing one off against the other, yet professing to be a dependable ally of all of them! Britain came to see him as wholly untrustworthy and consequently he came to place all his hopes in Napoleon III. Once again, in July 1857 at Plombières speaking to the Count de Salamar, Cavour's boyhood friend, the Emperor talked of a war with Austrian in alliance with Piedmont, but once again he did nothing about it. Patriots despaired of Napoleon's inaction and some decided to take drastic action (see page 53). Another setback for Cavour in 1857 was the Austrian emperor Franz Josef's adoption of a more reasonable policy in Lombardy. Radetzky was replaced by the liberal Archduke Maximilian and an amnesty for political offences was granted. Despite the fact that the Austrian Foreign Minister, Count Buol, subsequently broke off diplomatic relations with Turin for no good reason, it might be fair to conclude that by the end of 1857 Piedmont was no nearer dislodging Austrian rule than it had been five years earlier when Cavour had first come to power.

Analysis

So had Cavour failed in his first five years? We have to remember that his initial aims were to modernise Piedmont – to improve her economy, rationalise her bureaucracy, reduce the power of the Church and put constitutional government on a firm footing. By these means he intended to make Piedmont the indisputable leader of Italian affairs. In these matters, it seems, he was a success.

Despite the growth in debt (by 1859 up six-fold to 725 million lira in twelve years), the Piedmontese economy had really taken off. By the end of the decade the Piedmontese rail network comprised 47 per cent of the lines of the entire peninsula. Between 1850 and 1858 imports grew by 40 per cent and exports by 31 per cent. Piedmont had only 20 per cent of the population of Italy but was responsible for 39 per cent of imports and 27 per cent of exports. However, it is true that Piedmont's image of progress and modernity was a little exaggerated; as Cavour concentrated more on foreign affairs many reforms were watered down or abandoned (for example, civil marriage was abandoned and the nationalisation of the monasteries was the subject of compromise), but this was the price he had to pay for maintaining constitutional government, or rather for maintaining his not inconsiderable personal power. Indeed his control over both parliament and the King bear testimony to his great political skill. Survival in office was an achievement in itself. Parliament was to some extent controlled by bribery and corruption as between a third and a half of the deputies were given government jobs either centrally or locally. In addition, Cavour maintained power by a centre coalition, a marriage (*connubio*) of interests between a wide variety of centre left and centre right politicians. When this was under threat, as it was after the success of the far right in the elections of November 1857, Cavour was not above sacrificing friends and stooping to the dubious device of challenging the validity of the election of a quarter of the deputies! Cavour needed parliament to legitimate his rule and if he was unscrupulous, at least he was successful.

Victor Emmanuel II's powers remained considerable and his exercise of them often dubious (if intermittent). He imposed his ministers of war on all governments and dabbled in secret diplomacy with disastrous results (for example his correspondence with the Pope assuring him he would resist his government's policy of reducing Church power). He rid himself of d'Azeglio, and Cavour often held on to power by compromise (over civil marriage and the monasteries) or by pre-empting the King (over war in 1855). Victor Emmanuel's lack of education and coarse manners actually made him popular with his people and though he did not really like Cavour, he recognised his ability – and both men shared the desire to enlarge Piedmont and expel the Austrians. Cavour did well to control such a man.

In foreign affairs Cavour had been less successful. Clearly one of his aims was to make Piedmont the leading progressive state in the peninsula, something which he had largely achieved. It was certainly the case that other (progressive) Italians looked to Piedmont for leadership. However, his other aims – Piedmontese aggrandisement, expulsion of the Austrians, Italian independence and complete dominance of the peninsula – all seemed as far away as ever. Participation in the Crimean War had given some boost to Piedmontese prestige, a place at the top table and some discussion of Italian affairs, but nothing really concrete. Indeed, the future of

Piedmont had come to settle on the whims of the Emperor of France and he was a difficult man to read. Napoleon made many encouraging statements but did absolutely nothing about them. On the contrary, he was often obstructive. At the Congress of Paris he opposed the idea of Piedmont being represented and later he was reluctant for the Italian question to be discussed (both occurred at British insistence). Cavour tried a variety of approaches, including the despatch of his nineteen-year-old cousin, the sultry Comtesse di Castiglione, to seduce the Emperor. In this she was very successful but her influence over Napoleon's Italian policy was probably minimal (though her recollections would have us believe otherwise!). It is important to understand, then, that at this time Cavour was not in control of events; Italy's destiny did not rest with him at all – it rested with the Emperor Napoleon III.

Part B: The creation of a northern Italian kingdom, 1858–60

Orsini, January 1858

It was Napoleon's inactivity or perceived betrayal with regard to the Italian cause that led Felice Orsini, an ex-Mazzinian, and three accomplices to attempt an assassination of the Emperor. In January 1858, Orsini hoped that the Emperor's death would lead to the creation of another republic which would be more sympathetic to the Italian cause. Travelling from exile in England with three large bombs made in Birmingham, the assassins made their way to Paris and on 14 January, when the Emperor arrived at the opera, all three bombs were thrown at his carriage. The result was devastation and mayhem – the imperial carriage was riddled with 76 holes, both horses died, eight bystanders were killed and a further 150 wounded, but the Emperor escaped without a scratch! Cavour was understandably devastated by this assassination attempt, afraid that his long struggle to gain Napoleon's help had been ruined. Surprisingly the reverse occurred, but initially Napoleon was furious: he even threatened to ally with Austria and occupy Piedmont! Cavour responded by stating he would do whatever Napoleon required. Here was Napoleon's opportunity. The Emperor demanded a clear commitment to France, the repression of radicals and dissidents, and the censorship of all newspapers. Cavour to some extent complied.

Then in February, at the time of his trial, Orsini underwent a remarkable transformation, so remarkable in fact that it may well have been engineered by Napoleon himself. In court Orsini's lawyer read out a letter from the assassin in which he appealed for Napoleon's forgiveness, expressed repentance and pleaded with the Emperor to do something constructive for Italy, points he reiterated in another letter (3 March) just prior to his execution. Interestingly, the Emperor sent both letters to Cavour for publication in Turin (13 March) and throughout the peninsula. This event proved to be a remarkable turning point in the fortunes of Italy.

Subsequently, Napoleon let it be known through several intermediaries that he wished to discuss the Italian situation privately. It would appear he was finally ready to intervene in Italy and to act against Austria. But the question is why? The answer is not altogether clear. Did he fear another assassination attempt? This seems unlikely. Was he persuaded by Orsini's eloquence? This, too, seems unlikely given his previous track record. Was he amazed at his escape? Had he been spared by Providence to do something for Italy? This is certainly a possibility, but it is more likely that he saw a golden opportunity to create a new Napoleonic era in Italy. It seems that only when Napoleon could dictate terms to Cavour, did he become seriously interested in the fate of Italy. In addition, Britain was preoccupied with India and Austria was isolated. Here was an opportunity for Napoleon to replace Austrian influence in the Italian peninsula with that of France, and he was determined not to let it slip.

Plombières, July 1858

Accordingly, Napoleon summoned Cavour to the spa town of Plombières where the Prime Minister arrived incognito on 20 July. The meeting was so secret that not even the French Foreign Minister knew about it, though he warned Napoleon that Cavour had been spotted in the town! We have no record of their secret discussions other than Cavour's letter to the King which he wrote several days later – and to what extent this is reliable, is a moot point. Basically, the two conspirators cynically planned an aggressive war against the Austrians who had to be made out to be the aggressors. They were to be provoked, then driven out of Lombardy and Venetia, and Italy was to become a loose federation of four states:

1 Piedmont would gain Lombardy, Venetia, Parma and Modena (and possibly the Romagna) to form a Kingdom of Upper Italy.

2 Tuscany would obtain Umbria and the Marches to form a Kingdom of Central Italy.

3 The Pope would retain the area around Rome and be compensated for the loss of territory by being given the Presidency of the Confederation.

4 Naples would remain the same but Ferdinand might be replaced by Lucien Murat (the son of Napoleon I's loyal general who had ruled Naples from 1808 to 1815).

Napoleon would provide 200,000 soldiers (Piedmont 100,000) and have overall command. In return he requested Savoy and possibly Nice and a marriage alliance to link his dynasty with that of the ancient House of Savoy. This would entail the marriage of Napoleon's cousin, the 36-year-old philanderer Prince Jérôme, to Victor Emanuel's 15-year-old daughter Clotilde! Napoleon was quite obsessive about this last point. There was certainly no discussion of unification, something which would be against French interests, and on several subsequent occasions Cavour spoke of Ancona as the geographical limit of his ambitions (see Figure 3 on page 60).

This secret meeting was soon known about (not least because of Cavour's indiscretions), but no one knew of its content. Cavour exploited what (little) nationalism there was by calling for volunteers from all over Italy, and in December he made Garibaldi a major-general in the Piedmontese army. On New Year's Day 1859 Napoleon made a public remark about the deterioration of relations with Austria. Ten days later Victor Emmanuel opened parliament with an unexpectedly bellicose speech.

On 26 January 1859 a formal (again secret) treaty was signed between France and Piedmont which confirmed some of what Cavour wrote of at Plombières, but was in fact much less specific and much less generous (unless of course Cavour had exaggerated!). The territorial changes, for instance, were quite vague, stipulating only that Piedmont would make gains but not actually specifying them (though by implication the Papal Legations were excluded). There was no mention of a confederation under the Pope – in fact nothing was said about the rest of Italy at all. However, the treaty made clear that France was to get the county of Nice (quite a lot larger than just the town) and the Duchy of Savoy, Prince Jérôme was to marry Clotilde (this occurred at the end of January) and Piedmont was to pay for all French expenses. It was clearly an agreement much more favourable to France than to Piedmont.

By February 1859 Europe was becoming alarmed at the rise in tension. Cavour himself was in an excitable state but he had been unsuccessful in stirring up trouble throughout the rest of Italy. The National Society was 'more of a propaganda organisation than an instrument for instigating practical agitation' (Mack Smith, 1985), though it did raise 10,000 volunteers. Napoleon was disappointed by the lack of disaffection and began to lose his nerve. When, early in March, some of the terms of the treaty got out and Prussia announced it would side with Austria, Napoleon decided on a postponement.

In mid-March Russia proposed a congress to resolve the tension; Britain and France immediately agreed. However, the French Foreign Minister did not even want Piedmont represented! The powers now tried to get Austria and Piedmont to 'disarm' (i.e. demobilise) and when a request came from Napoleon on 17 April to do just that, Cavour was so depressed he threatened to shoot himself. At this point the Austrians played right into his hands and he was able 'to snatch war from the jaws of peace'! Count Buol now erroneously believed the Piedmontese had lost French backing and made the mistake of concluding that the moment had come to teach the Piedmontese a lesson and end these provocations. In addition, he did not want Austria to appear weak and have to treat Piedmont as an equal at the congress. He wanted a diplomatic or military victory prior to it. If it came to war he expected a quick victory and in any event could no longer afford to bear the cost of mobilisation. Thus, on 21 April, the Austrians sent an ultimatum to Piedmont demanding demobilisation; on 26 April Cavour rejected this and war followed. This ultimatum placed Austria entirely in the wrong in the eyes of Europe. Piedmont was now the victim. Ironically, then, the Austrians made themselves the aggressors despite Napoleon and Cavour's best efforts. It could not have worked out better for Cavour.

War: April–July 1859

Fortunately for Piedmont the war got off to a very slow start. The Austrians had to move quickly to occupy Turin before French forces arrived if they were going to win, but General Gyulai lacked Radetzky's brilliance and moved far too slowly. He only crossed the border on 29 April and was slowed by heavy rain. He then adopted a defensive, static posture and allowed the French to arrive – Napoleon had declared war on 3 May – and build up their forces. The Austrians had about 220,000 soldiers in all; France initially provided 110,000, but Piedmont was only able to recruit about 60,000.

As early as 27 April a mass demonstration in Tuscany (not organised by the National Society) led to the Grand Duke's exile. A provisional government was formed by Baron Bettino Ricasoli who offered Victor Emmanuel temporary control, but, significantly, Napoleon would not allow this to happen. Elsewhere the National Society was unable to produce risings and further developments only occurred after the first Austrian defeat. This took place at the battle of Magenta on 4 June. This three hour battle was such a bloody affair that it gave the world a new word for a new colour. The battle was not decisive, though it might have been so had the Piedmontese turned up on time (they arrived after it was all over!). Subsequently, the Austrians pulled their garrisons out of Bologna, Ancona, Pavia, Piacenza and Ferrara (i.e. Modena, Parma and the Papal States) and the dukes of Parma and Modena fled. Cavour sent in troops and royal commissioners to liaise with National Society members and organise pro-Piedmontese governments in the duchies. Luigi Carlo Farini was made Governor of Modena on 19 June and Victor Emmanuel despatched troops to the Romagna with d'Azeglio in charge. But again Napoleon blocked the Romagna's absorption by Piedmont; he did not want to upset the Pope, and he did not want Piedmont expanding into the central duchies.

A second massive battle occurred on 24 June at Solferino involving over 300,000 men. Again the slaughter was on a colossal scale – the Austrians suffered 22,000 casualties, the French 17,000 and the Piedmontese 5,000 – and it prompted a Swiss observer, Henri Dunant, to found the Red Cross. Although this was another (expensive) French victory and the Austrians retreated to the fortresses of the Quadrilateral, ultimate victory appeared to be a long way off – the Austrians still had an army of 150,000, they occupied all of Venetia and the fortresses would be difficult to reduce. Even before this battle Napoleon was becoming disillusioned with the war, as well as by the lack of popular support and by Cavour's deceits over Tuscany and the Papal States. It was becoming obvious to him that Piedmont was simply not going to be a French satellite. On 3 July the French formally complained that Cavour's ambitions in Central Italy were damaging the alliance. In addition, the Emperor was frustrated by the poor Piedmontese performance in terms of both organisation and military effectiveness. Inadequate food supplies held up the armies and fortresses could not be besieged because the siege artillery had been left behind in Turin.

If Napoleon was not going to establish French hegemony over the peninsula, he might as well call the war off – and that is just what he did. On 5 July he asked for an armistice and on 8 July a five-week truce was agreed. There were a number of other reasons why Napoleon called the war off at this time, apart from Cavour's double-dealing. The Emperor was himself horrified by the carnage and realised the price of victory would be too high and take too long. In addition, the war was already very unpopular in France and, more importantly, on 24 June the Prussians mobilised along the Rhine, presenting the Emperor with the possibility of a two-front war.

King Victor Emmanuel was initially quite happy for the armistice to be turned into a full peace. However, Cavour unrealistically felt Piedmont should continue the war alone. He was overruled. On 11 July Napoleon and Franz Josef, the Austrian emperor, met at Villafranca (without any Piedmontese representative) to talk peace. The emperors agreed to the creation of an Italian confederation under the Pope and the cession of Lombardy to Piedmont (see Figure 3). Napoleon did not claim either Nice or Savoy but he did want payment (the war had already cost some 350 million francs!). The emperors also stated that the dukes of

Modena and Tuscany should be restored, though without stipulating how; restoration was not wanted by the people of the duchies.

When Cavour heard of this arrangement, he went berserk. He caused a terrible scene and turned deep purple; he may even have had a mental breakdown. He also resigned (11 July). But the situation was not as bad as all that, as he himself was to recognise a few days afterwards. The key to the future lay in the duchies. Cavour had actually achieved more than he realised.

The duchies: July 1859–March 1860

After the armistice, the Piedmontese commissioners and troops had to withdraw from the central duchies. Farini managed to retain his authority by resigning as Piedmontese Governor and assuming dictatorial powers by popular acclamation in Modena on 27 July, and in Parma on 18 August. In Florence the Governor Ricasoli, who did not have to resign because he was a Tuscan noble, organised elections. The resultant parliament voted on 20 August for annexation by Piedmont (pending Napoleon III's approval). Similarly, the assembly in Modena also voted for annexation on 21 August, as did the Romagna on 6 and 7 September and Parma on 12 September. In addition, on 31 October Modena, Parma and the Romagna united as Emilia under the control of Farini. However, Napoleon III was not in favour of annexation (he stated, 'I will not have unity') and he put pressure on Victor Emmanuel to refuse. Italian liberty and unity were obviously not at the top of his agenda. However, after Villafranca he was clearly losing influence. At the same time Britain took a very positive line about further Piedmontese expansion and Palmerston explicitly opposed the return of the dukes to the central duchies. When the Treaty of Zurich was signed between France and Austria on 10 November 1859, little was finalised apart from the transfer of Lombardy to Piedmont. The matters of the restoration of the old order to the central duchies and the confederation under the Pope were to be the subject of discussion at a congress in Paris in January 1860.

Then in December 1859 Napoleon III changed his mind about the settlement. He realised it would be impossible to enforce Villafranca, particularly now that Britain supported Piedmontese annexation, and he was embarrassed at his failure to obtain anything for France after all

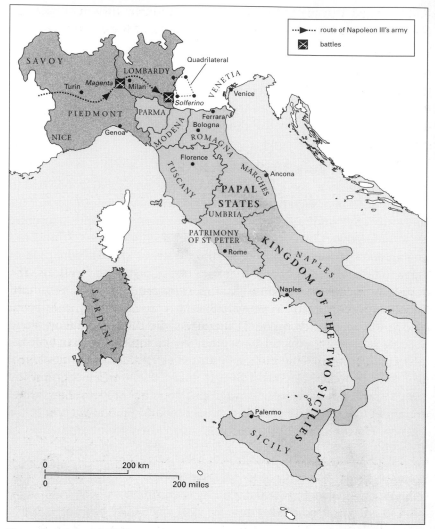

Figure 3 Italy in July 1859

the sacrifices of the war. Accordingly, he let it be known that the Pope might not be able to hold on to the Romagna and he privately indicated his wish to obtain Nice and Savoy if a deal could be struck. As a result, Austria would not take part in any congress and when Lord John Russell, the British Foreign Secretary, made a proposal in January 1860 that the powers should adopt a policy of non-intervention in

Italian affairs and allow the Italians to determine their own future, Napoleon agreed (as eventually did a reluctant Austria). The scene was set for a new settlement.

However, since July Cavour had been out of office – a situation that the King relished – and his successor, General Lamarmora, had not infused Piedmont with decisive leadership. With Napoleon's change of direction Cavour was now determined to return to power and he conducted a forceful campaign in the press. Aided by the support of the British ambassador, Sir James Hudson, and the outgoing ministers, Cavour returned as Prime Minister on 20 January. The King reluctantly agreed to his appointment (on the understanding that he promised not to discuss the monarch's private life). He returned not only as Prime Minister, but as Foreign Minister and Minister of the Interior as well.

There followed six weeks of difficult negotiations with Napoleon. Cavour wanted Modena, Parma, the Romagna and Tuscany but Napoleon was reluctant to allow the latter – Tuscany had never been part of the original deal. The Emperor wanted Nice and Savoy; they were natural frontiers for France and would justify the sacrifices of 1859, but whereas Savoy was largely French, that was not the case with Nice. However, Britain was opposed to French annexations, Victor Emmanuel was not happy to give up Savoy and Italians in general were not happy at the sacrifice of any territory, especially that of Nice.

At last agreement was reached on the basis of plebiscites in each of the areas and Cavour went ahead without consulting parliament. The votes in Emilia and Tuscany were held on 11 and 12 March 1860 and resulted in overwhelming majorities in favour of annexation (427,512 votes for, 756 against and 386,445 for, 14,925 against, respectively; see Figure 4). The voting was well organised or an absurd farce, as an English observer put it, depending upon your point of view. Clearly there were some irregularities – more votes than voters – and a somewhat liberal dispensation of free wine, but it does appear that a majority felt they were in favour of King Victor Emmanuel and Piedmont, whatever that might mean.

As far as Nice and Savoy were concerned, Napoleon III made it clear that these territories were non-negotiable and on 12 March, Victor

Figure 4 Italy in March 1860

Emmanuel signed them away prior to the plebiscites. The latter took place between 15 and 22 April under the watchful eye of French soldiers and were patently fraudulent. In Savoy, 130,583 voted in favour, 235 against; in Nice, 24,448 in favour, 160 against (the formal transfer occurred in June).

Cavour faced a lot of criticism in the new parliament (it had been suspended during the war) and he was clearly embarrassed at having to defend what had happened. It caused a breach with Garibaldi who was born in Nice. The Prime Minister lost the argument but won the vote since parliament saw that what had happened was politically necessary. However, Cavour's reputation was badly tarnished by this whole affair.

On 16 April, Cavour went to Florence – he had never been so far south – to celebrate the annexation of Tuscany. However, this was not a happy event as the King constantly criticised him for giving up Nice and for failing to obtain Ancona, and showed greater favour to Ricasoli, who was now clearly a rival. Cavour could not believe his monarch's ingratitude.

So, despite having achieved what he set out to achieve – an enlarged Piedmont (Victor Emmanuel now ruled half the Italian population and one-third of its territory) – all this success did not bring Cavour much immediate satisfaction. Still, his work was largely done; apart from Venetia and papal territory he had no thoughts of further expansion. There was certainly no discussion of unification; this was something for a later generation. Then a revolt broke out in Palermo in April, and the situation transformed yet again.

Analysis

So, what were Cavour's aims and what did he achieve? As we indicated in our analysis in Part A of this chapter (see page 45), Cavour set out to modernise Piedmont and make her the leader of Italy. This, to some extent, he achieved. However, with regard to his aims to free Italy from Austrian control and to enlarge Piedmont, he had not made any progress up to 1858. Attempts to woo Napoleon III had failed. Then, remarkably, between 1858 and 1860 he was able to achieve all his aims. He enlarged Piedmont and reduced Austrian influence. How was he able to do this? The truth is of course that these were not actually Cavour's achievements at all, but rather the unexpected result of Napoleon's designs coupled with a good deal of luck. This is not to demean or dismiss Cavour in any way; it is simply to recognise that we are all to some extent dependent on the actions of others.

Cavour had no knowledge of Orsini's bomb and yet this assassination attempt proved to be the main turning point in modern Italian history. However, Napoleon did not see it as a sign from God to liberate Italy, but rather as an opportunity to enhance French interests and dominate the peninsula. Thus it was that the Emperor summoned Cavour to Plombières (not the other way round) and in effect dictated terms to him which involved a dynastic marriage and the cession of territory to France. The treaty of January 1859 was much nearer the truth than Cavour's report of July 1858.

Napoleon soon lost his nerve and it appeared Cavour would not get his war until the Austrians played right into his hands. This happened by pure chance. As d'Azeglio put it, 'It was one of those jackpots you win only once in a century.' But the war did not go to plan for either Napoleon or Cavour. Indeed, the war proved to be both indecisive and decisive at the same time. Indecisive in the sense that it had reached a stalemate and in the sense that France had not replaced Austria as the dominant power in Italy; decisive in the sense that Austrian control over the peninsula was in effect now broken, and in the sense that a political vacuum had been created into which the Piedmontese could now step. The result was a fluid situation with potential for Piedmontese expansion but little return for France. However, it was Napoleon's war – he fought it and he called it off and he would decide the outcome. He did not even invite a Piedmontese to discuss the peace settlement. He was actually concerned to keep Piedmont in check. But a certain momentum for Piedmontese expansion had built up, though even Cavour was unaware of the progress that had been made in the central duchies. This was largely the work of Ricasoli and Farini, but when Cavour returned to office in January 1860, he was able to respond to Napoleon's change of policy and achieve a settlement. The compromise that was achieved – the annexation of the central duchies by Piedmont in return for the transfer of Nice and Savoy to France – was not exactly what either party had hoped for, but it offered something to each. Napoleon was not going to dominate the peninsula but at least he got some territory (the annexations made him very popular in France), and Cavour obtained his Kingdom of Upper Italy even if Venetia remained in Austrian hands.

Events might have stopped there. Neither party, it must be emphasised, was interested in unification. A united Italy would damage French interests; Napoleon wanted a French satellite as a neighbour, not a strong state. And Cavour was not really interested in the Italian cause. As the British ambassador in Paris observed in March 1859, Italian liberty did not seem uppermost in his mind, but rather hatred of Austria, personal ambition and a thirst for Piedmontese aggrandisement. He often talked of Ancona as the geographical limit of his ambitions – he knew nothing of the south and felt that unity was something for another generation. Garibaldi, on the other hand, felt that unity could be achieved immediately, and it was he who took the initiative.

Notemaking

A few tips

As you are probably already aware, notemaking is the **foundation** of all your study activity. The notes you make act as a reminder of what you have read. They also (often) form the basis for essay writing and (usually) for revision. Moreover, notemaking makes reading **an active** process as you are required to concentrate and extract the most important points.

The two most common errors when notemaking are either writing out too much – there is no point in writing out practically the whole book – or too little, thereby missing out important points. Proper notemaking requires you to think hard about what is relevant and this can be quite difficult when you are unfamiliar with a topic. It is best to read through a chapter in its entirety first to put the content in perspective, rather than make notes as you go along.

Another useful tip is to ensure that your notes are **easy on the eye**. A densely packed set of words is rather off-putting when it is time for revision. It is important to space out your notes and break up the pages with gaps (these can be useful for extra points later). Always indent, and use headings, subheadings, numbered points, underlining, colours, etc. Above all make your notes interesting. Of course, notemaking is a personal matter and you should end up with an approach that best suits you.

Making notes on this chapter

This chapter already has a number of headings which can be used to divide up your notes:

Part A: Cavour, Piedmont and the leadership of Italy, 1850–7
1 Background: **a** Piedmont **b** Cavour
2 Cavour in office – the early years
3 Cavour and the Crimean War
4 Cavour and the National Society
5 Analysis

Part B: The creation of a northern Italian kingdom, 1858–60
1 Orsini, January 1858
2 Plombières, July 1858
3 War: April–July 1859

4 The duchies, July 1859–March 1860

5 Analysis

Documentary exercise (1859)

◢ Document A

Frenchmen, Austria in ordering her army to invade the territory of the King of Sardinia, our ally, has declared war upon us. Piedmont having accepted conditions which should have maintained peace, one cannot but inquire what can be the reason for this sudden invasion on Austria's part.

The purpose of this war is then to restore Italy to herself, not simply to change her master; and we shall have upon our frontiers a friendly people who will owe their independence to us. We are not going into Italy to foment disorder, not to disturb the authority of the Holy Father, whom we have replaced upon his throne but to protect him against foreign aggression which weighs upon the whole peninsula, and to participate in establishing order there which shall satisfy all legitimate interests. We are in short about to enter that classic land rendered illustrious by so many victories. We shall find there the traces of our forefathers, of whom God grant we may prove ourselves worthy.

> *Napoleon III explains why he is about to intervene in the Italian question,*
> *reported in **Le Moniteur**, 4 May 1859*

◢ Document B

Between His Majesty the Emperor of Austria and His Majesty the Emperor of the French it has been agreed as follows.

1. *The Two Sovereigns favour the creation of an Italian Confederation. This Confederation shall be under the honorary Presidency of the Holy Father.*

2. *The Emperor of Austria cedes to the Emperor of the French his rights over Lombardy with the exception of the Fortressess of Mantua and Peschiera.*

3. *The Emperor of the French shall present the ceded Territory to the King of Sardinia.*

4. *Venetia shall form part of the Italian Confederation, remaining, however, subject to the Crown of the Emperor of Austria.*

5. *The Grand Duke of Tuscany and the Duke of Modena shall return to their States, granting a general Amnesty.*

6. *The Two Emperors shall request the Holy Father to introduce in his States some indispensable reforms.*

> *From the Preliminary Treaty of Villafranca, 11 July 1859*

◢ Document C

The people of the Duchies have elected representative assemblies, and these assemblies have unanimously and by vote by ballot, declared the deposal of the former dynasties and a determination of a union with Piedmont. The two Emperors, being the principal belligerent parties, might claim for themselves the right of disposing of the territories which were the seat and prize of war – Piedmont, Lombardy and Venetia – but they have no right to dispose of the future destiny of other parts of Italy.

England is one of the great powers of Europe, and must take part in European deliberations. Viscount Palmerston would beg to submit that there are two systems of Policy which might be followed in regard to the present state of things in Italy. The one an Austrian, the other an Italian system of policy. The Austrian Policy would lead to the restoration, and if possible the augmentation of Austrian supremacy in Italy. This supremacy and domination of Austria has for a long course of years been the cause of infinite misery, social, civil and political, to the nations of Italy.

The Italian system of Policy, on the contrary, would tend to free the people of Italy from the thraldom of foreign control and leave them at full liberty to decide for themselves what should be their internal organisation and their condition of political existence.

From a letter from Lord Palmerston, the British Prime Minister, to Queen Victoria, 6 August 1859

1 What reasons does Napoleon III give in Document A for entering the war against Austria in 1859? *4 marks*

2 What circumstances led to Austria's 'sudden invasion' (Document A) of Sardinia in 1859? *6 marks*

3 Compare the value of Documents A and C as sources for French and British policy during the Italian crisis of 1859, and comment on the extent to which these reveal a conflict of interests. *7 marks*

4 How far do the documents show why the preliminary peace of Villafranca failed to provide a lasting settlement of the Italian question? *8 marks*

OCR (formerly Oxford Delegacy), 1987

Chapter Four

GARIBALDI AND UNIFICATION – ACCIDENT OR DESIGN?

Objectives
◢ To consider how Garibaldi took advantage of the Sicilian uprising
◢ To consider his success in Naples
◢ To understand how unification came about
◢ To determine the role of the key individuals in the process.

Background

Giuseppe Garibaldi was one of those historical figures who possessed that elusive quality, charisma, and for a while must have been the most widely known figure in the world. He was the archetypal romantic hero, the swashbuckling adventurer who was able to command the devotion of both men and women. He was admired for his honesty and integrity, and his humble origins and way of life provided him with an understanding of ordinary people that was itself one reason for many of his successes. Moreover, he was unconventional for his age and believed strongly in personal freedom, for himself and for his followers. His unconventionality made him both admired by the common folk and feared by the establishment.

As we have seen in the Picture Gallery (page 9), Garibaldi was born in Nice in 1807 and became totally committed to Italian unification after his meeting with Mazzini in 1833. Ten adventurous years of sailing in the Mediterranean and the Black Sea were followed by ten years of exile in South America where, among other things, he was a spaghetti salesman! In addition he became a soldier, acquired the techniques of guerrilla warfare and helped form the state of Uruguay. However, the most important part of his career began after 1848, when he was over the age of 40. We have already referred to his defence of the Roman Republic in 1849 (pages 35 and 39), his return from exile in 1854 (when he saw that the Piedmontese monarchy was a more realistic vehicle for the Italian cause than republican revolution), and his participation in the war with Austria). Although Cavour made him a major-general in the Piedmontese army, he was sidelined with only 3,300 volunteers in a difficult, but successful, Alpine campaign. He was sidelined because he was considered potentially dangerous and was not really trusted. As we have also seen (page 63), he broke with Cavour over the cession of Nice, his birthplace, and he was determined to reverse the decision. He was deeply unhappy with the outcome of the war.

The Sicilian uprising

Garibaldi's reaction to the cession of Nice was to contemplate a military expedition to prevent the annexation taking place. With this in mind, he began to form the volunteer force that was to become the 'Thousand'. At the same time, Sicily broke out into revolt. The rising which began in Palermo on 4 April was soon suppressed, but subsequently other risings began to occur throughout the island. These were mainly peasant uprisings, social in character, but they had the effect of breaking down local government and Bourbon control. Here then was an opportunity. These events had the fortunate effect of persuading Garibaldi to abandon his unrealistic plan for Nice and concentrate on the island of Sicily. Thus he went to support a revolt, not to initiate it – he was reacting to events rather than creating them. But his goal was unification.

Garibaldi sailed from Genoa on 5–6 May in two small paddle steamers with slightly more than a thousand poorly armed volunteers, who mainly consisted of young professionals, students and urban workers from the north of Italy. Although Garibaldi announced that they would fight under the banner of 'Victor Emmanuel and Italy', Cavour feared the diplomatic repercussions. He was in fact opposed to the expedition, but Garibaldi's prestige and the patriotic mood was such that any attempt at stopping the Thousand Red Shirts would have been politically impossible, though he did issue an order to have the paddle steamers detained if they put into Sardinian waters. In any event, the Piedmontese Prime Minister did not expect Garibaldi to succeed, and took the view that in the unlikely event that the expedition was successful, he would be able to take advantage of the situation.

However, the outcome was remarkable beyond the wildest romantic dream and Cavour was to lose the initiative to Garibaldi for the rest of the summer.

Garibaldi's conquest of Sicily with a thousand men against a Neapolitan army of 25,000 astonished contemporaries and even now is difficult to explain. He landed at Marsala unopposed on 11 May because, it is believed, the Neapolitan soldiers nearby mistook the red shirts of his volunteer force for British forces! On 14 May Garibaldi declared himself the 'Dictator' of Sicily (this did not have the pejorative twentieth-century connotation; it simply referred to temporary emergency authority) and the following day he won a difficult, small-scale but decisive victory at Calatafimi. The psychological impact of this victory was immense and it persuaded the islanders of Garibaldi's invincibility. Large numbers of volunteers now swelled his ranks, though it should be recognised that Sicilian 'patriots' were inspired by the wish for independence and hatred of landlords and Bourbon government – not a desire for Italian unification. Still, Garibaldi's courage, sincerity and honesty won him the devotion of the people. 'There is magic in his look and in his name,' as Giuseppe Abba, one of the Thousand, put it.

After a cunning false attack had drawn some of the garrison away, Garibaldi entered Palermo, the capital, on 27 May. The Bourbon troops, the bulk of whom were in the capital, remained in the fortress and the viceroy, Ferdinand Lanza, decided to seek an armistice (30 May). Given that the island was now slipping into chaos and he had no instructions, Lanza decided to negotiate an evacuation (7 June) and on 19 June the Neapolitan garrison steamed away in 24 ships. After the battle of Milazzo on 20 July, and once he took Messina on 27 July, Garibaldi faced no further Bourbon resistance, and the island was his to control. Even Cavour had to acknowledge this achievement:

◢ Source

Garibaldi has rendered Italy the greatest services that a man could give her: he has given Italians confidence in themselves: he has proved to Europe that Italians know how to fight and die on the battlefield to reconquer a fatherland.

*Quoted by H. Hearder in **Cavour** (Longman, 1994)*

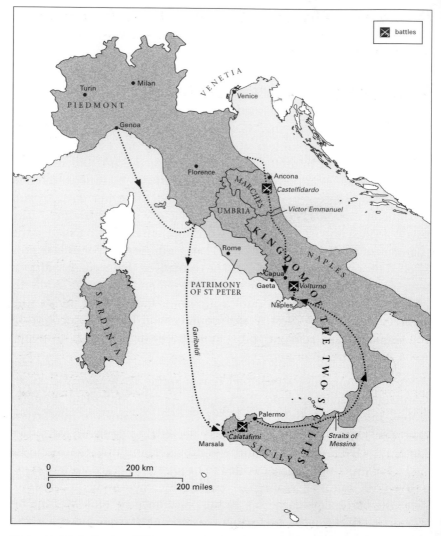

Figure 5 Italy in October 1860

At this point the alliance with the peasants began to break down and Garibaldi found himself siding with the men of property, the land-owners, in order to restore law and order. He was not going to allow a social revolution to get in the way of his political goals. Cavour desperately tried to regain the initiative by arranging a quick annexation. However, Garibaldi would not hear of it. He wanted to keep Sicily as a base for his next campaign – against the Bourbon monarchy on the mainland.

The conquest of Naples

Insurrections had already broken out in Calabria and Basilicata in anticipation of Garibaldi's arrival. Cavour was wholly opposed to a mainland campaign (as indeed was Napoleon III) and initially tried to negotiate an alliance with King Francis II. When this failed, he attempted to foment a revolution in Naples, but this was also unsuccessful. In any event, Garibaldi was able to undertake two successful crossings between 18 and 21 August despite this opposition. This was to some extent due to the goodwill of the British Mediterranean Fleet, whose support largely negated any Piedmontese or French naval threat.

After Garibaldi's landing, spontaneous revolts in peasant villages and towns destroyed the power of the Bourbon police and administration and led to the defection of many soldiers. Wherever he went, Garibaldi was greeted with popular acclaim, '*Il nostro secondo Gesu Cristo*' (Our second Jesus Christ!) being just one of the (more extreme) assessments. His advance from Calabria up to Naples became a triumphal procession as he was virtually unopposed.

The 24-year-old Francis II, who had only been king for just over a year, was not the right person to handle this emergency. Already in June he had granted a constitution, but by replacing loyal monarchist ministers with unreliable liberal ones he had in fact weakened his government still further. When an insurrection occurred in the city of Naples itself, Francis ordered his 50,000 strong army north to the fortress at Capua and he himself sailed north to Gaeta. Thus the city of Naples was abandoned and Garibaldi was able to go ahead of his forces by train and capture it with a mere 30 colleagues (7 September)! Cavour was by now a very worried man as he feared Garibaldi would remain dictator of Naples and not hand over his conquests. Already in August he had written:

◢ Source

If Garibaldi passes to the Continent and establishes himself and his capital in the Kingdom of Naples as he has done in Sicily, he becomes absolute master of the situation. King Victor Emmanuel loses almost all his prestige; in the eyes of the great majority of Italians he will become only the friend of Garibaldi. He will probably keep the crown, but this crown will shine only as a reflection of what a heroic adventurer judges good to shine on it. Garibaldi will not proclaim the republic at Naples; but he will not carry out annexation and he will keep the dictatorship. He will dispose of the resources of a kingdom of 9,000,000 inhabitants, and will be surrounded by an irresistible prestige. We will not be able to struggle against him.

Quoted by H. Hearder in **Cavour** (Longman, 1994)

However, despite his fear, Cavour was about to regain the initiative by finally embracing unification.

Garibaldi announced that he intended to march on Rome (he had named his ugliest donkey on Caprera, *Pio Nono* – Pius IX!), then Venice, then Nice. Cavour feared that this would lead to a clash with France and might well undo all he had achieved thus far. However, he was able to use Garibaldi's intentions to play on French fears and persuade Napoleon of his plan to intervene in the south. Napoleon for his part was increasingly alarmed at Garibaldi's open expressions of hostility towards France and was not unhappy at Cavour's suggestion. Thus we can see that Cavour was in effect forced into unifying Italy just to stop Garibaldi.

In late August, Piedmontese officials met with the Emperor in Savoy to inform him of the plan which would also involve annexing Umbria and the Marches but leave the Pope in charge of the area around Rome. Napoleon could not publicly support an attack on Papal territory, but privately he stated, 'Do it, but do it quickly.' Cavour's great gamble was about to pay off. However, although he moved quickly, it did not all go according to plan. The Piedmontese Prime Minister had to pretend he was entering the Papal States to restore order, but the pretext of unrest foundered when the unrest proved to be insignificant. Still, the invasion went ahead. The 33,000 strong Piedmontese army crossed the border on 11 September and though the Papal army put up considerable resistance, it did not stand a chance. It was in fact only about one-third the size of the Piedmontese force and succumbed at the battle of Castelfidardo on 18 September. Now, finally, Cavour announced that Piedmont favoured a unitary solution to the Italian question, and with the capture of Ancona on 29 September the way was clear to either link up with Garibaldi or confront him.

In fact Garibaldi had not really been in a position to march on Rome at all – the 50,000 strong Neapolitan army was in the way, and although he defeated it at Volturno (1–2 October) he suffered great losses and was considerably weakened militarily. Indeed, given the fact that the Neapolitans were still not completely defeated, and also the fact that peasant risings in the south were already getting out of control, Garibaldi needed the Piedmontese army to finish the job. Accordingly, he requested Victor Emmanuel's assistance. Thus Cavour did not prevent Garibaldi's march on Rome, the Neapolitans did.

Now in October, Victor Emmanuel joined his army in the Papal States and it was clear that Piedmont had regained the initiative. Cavour was able to intervene in the south to thwart democratically elected local assemblies and impose one-off plebiscites instead. Moreover, no mention was made of annexation to Piedmont; voters were simply required to vote in favour of (or oppose) 'Italia Una Vittorio Emanuele' – the slogan under which Garibaldi had fought. The votes on 21 October registered overwhelming approval for the proposition, though in truth they were more an expression of admiration for Garibaldi than anything else. In Naples 1,302,064 voted 'yes', 10,302 'no'; in Sicily 432,053 voted 'yes', 667 'no'.

On 20 October Garibaldi and Victor Emmanuel finally met at Teano, near Capua, where Garibaldi agreed to hand over his conquests. This was undoubtedly an act of selfless patriotic generosity, but given Garibaldi's weakened military position, it is probably true to say that he really had little choice in the matter.

The Piedmontese army finally took Capua on 2 November and though Francis II held out in Gaeta until February 1861, to all intents and purposes the campaign was over. Then, on 7 November, Victor Emmanuel and Garibaldi made a formal entry into Naples, though the latter was embarrassed by the crowds shouting 'Viva Garibaldi!' when he felt they should be shouting 'Viva il Re!' (Long live the King).

The King and Garibaldi got on well, but Victor Emmanuel was firm with Garibaldi and told him his army of irregulars had to be disbanded. Garibaldi himself refused all honours and gifts including the title of prince and a castle, not least in protest about the shabby treatment of his soldiers, and left for his rocky homeland of Caprera on 9 November with little more than a year's supply of macaroni!

Previously, on 4 November plebiscites in the Marches and Umbria had registered overwhelming 'yes' votes for union (133,765 vs. 1,212; and 97,040 vs. 360 respectively). None of the Great Powers had intervened though a large number of countries disapproved, including Austria and Russia. Napoleon gave secret approval but it was only Great Britain that gave public approval. Cavour had taken a great risk, but it had paid off.

On 27 January 1861 elections took place for the first parliament of Italy, which met on 18 February. Victor Emmanuel was finally proclaimed King of Italy on 17 March 1861 after Francis had given up and abdicated. Italy had come into being at last. But not everything was rosy in the garden. Cavour's attempts to acquire Rome by negotiation got nowhere (despite the offer of a fifteen million lira bribe to the Papal secretary of state), and the south was slipping into civil war. The Prime Minister was now determined to maintain unity at all costs and this translated into a growing rejection of any form of *devolution*. Central control would have to be imposed. At this crucial and difficult time Cavour suddenly died, on 6 June 1861, of 'fever' (probably malaria), leaving the new Italy without an obvious leader. He was only 50 years old and his political skill would be missed. The new kingdom faced a myriad of problems.

KEY TERM

Devolution is the delegation of power from central to local or regional administration.

Analysis

So was Italy unified by accident or design? Quite clearly in the case of Garibaldi it was a matter of design. Of all the major protagonists he alone was committed to a united Italy from start to finish. Napoleon was not; Cavour was not, and Victor Emmanuel was too much of a realist to consider it a possibility. Yet even in the case of Garibaldi, accident played a large role. For one thing, he did not initiate the revolt in Sicily – that this occurred when it did was quite fortuitous. Moreover, the revolt itself was not an uprising in the name of a united Italy; the Sicilians were notorious separatists and wanted independence. The peasants were reacting to the oppression of the landlords and simply wanted land redistribution. There is no doubt that Garibaldi's campaign was 'one of the most extraordinary victories won by an ill-equipped guerrilla force in the history of warfare' (Grenville, 1976), but he was greatly helped by the Sicilians who threw the island into complete chaos, and by the incompetence of the Neapolitans. The bulk of the garrison (20,000 out of 25,000) was bottled up in Palermo and the viceroy, Lanza, took the first opportunity to give up and get out. Clearly, given their numerical superiority, the Neapolitans could have and should have dealt with Garibaldi's irregular band. The fact that they did not was largely due to the spineless performance of the incompetent Lanza.

However, Lanza's incompetence was merely a reflection of the incompetence of the entire regime. The mainland campaign was not dissimilar to that of the island campaign. The peasants rose up, chaos ensued, the King retreated and the government gave up. Some would say (Gladstone in particular) that it was a fitting end to a rotten dynasty! But once again we should not, by stating all this, in any way demean Garibaldi's remarkable achievement. His personal qualities and military skill translated into popular support and military success. However, it is interesting to note that when he tried to repeat this sort of campaign in 1862 and 1867, and came up against determined opposition, he was easily stopped.

Garibaldi was a man of principle. He did not conquer Bourbon Naples for himself but for Victor Emmanuel and Italy. However, when the people of the south came to vote, it is not clear that they knew what they were voting for. Many were illiterate and some thought *Italia* was the King's wife! The vote was largely a vote for Garibaldi, not his ideal.

Garibaldi, then, is fundamental to the unification process. Fundamental in another way too, because it was he who forced Cavour to embrace unification. Cavour himself, as we have already noted, knew nothing of the south, never went south of Florence and aimed at an enlarged Piedmont stretching only as far south as Ancona. He did not envisage full unification until a much later date, possibly by another generation. However, Garibaldi's phenomenal success transformed the situation. Cavour was opposed to his expedition and, after his conquest of Sicily, was opposed to the mainland campaign. He did not see Garibaldi's work as part of a great process of unification, but as a threat to everything he had achieved. He could not believe Garibaldi was a man of principle and would hand over his conquests; and he could not believe Austria and France would stand idly by while Garibaldi marched up the peninsula, in particular to Rome. He had to be stopped. And the only way this could be done was by conquering part of the Papal States and taking over the southern kingdom.

Cavour unified Italy not because he believed in a united Italy but to stop Garibaldi. It was a desperate gamble to preserve an enlarged Piedmont – and it succeeded in enlarging Piedmont still further!

Of course, once he had achieved unification he became a firm advocate of it and subsequently he was dubbed its architect. However, this was not true. Cavour was not a planner, but he was a great opportunist. He himself stated that 'everything depends on accident'. The alliance with France was not of his making. That this alliance created opportunities for Piedmont was as much to do with Napoleon's lack of resolve and Austria's subsequent weakness as it was to do with Cavour's talent and foresight, and, as we have seen, unification itself was forced upon him by Garibaldi's remarkable achievements.

◢ Source

That his schemes succeeded owed more to luck than to design. But in politics Cavour was always blessed with immense good fortune. Even the timing of his death, less than three months after Victor Emmanuel had been crowned King of Italy, was fortuitous – sparing him the enormous problems and disappointments which trailed in the wake of unification.

*Nick Carter, 'Rethinking Cavour', in **Modern History Review**, November 1997*

When Cavour died, Palmerston described him as 'one of the greatest patriots that has ever adorned the history of any nation', but more accurate was Lord Acton's assessment; he described Cavour's achievements as 'a triumph of unscrupulous statesmanship'. Still, his work outlived his death – Italy remained a constitutional monarchy for some considerable time. And the real measure of his achievement can be seen in the decade that followed his death when nine prime ministers came and went in quick succession. None of them had his political skill and strength of character, none of them could hold on to office for any length of time.

What of the role of the other two protagonists, Napoleon III and Victor Emmanuel?

The French Emperor had hoped to dominate the Italian peninsula but his ambitions took a tumble at the first hurdle. He did obtain his marriage alliance and he did obtain Nice and Savoy, but the effect of his campaign was to nullify Austria's power and create a vacuum in the peninsula into which the Italians themselves were able to step. Without the deaths of so many French soldiers, Italian unification could not have come about. However, after July 1859 Napoleon became something of a spectator, though not a passive one, as Cavour felt he could never proceed without the Emperor's approval. How likely Napoleon's intervention was over the central duchies or the Kingdom of Naples is a moot point. Cavour thought he would intervene, but the unpopularity of the war in France, and British and Prussian opposition to French ambitions were such that any intervention was probably unlikely. Napoleon had started a process which he had not wanted, but now he had to give it his blessing.

King Victor Emmanuel, who rather pointedly styled himself 'The Second' of Italy, keeping his Piedmontese designation, was something of an enigma. He too, like Cavour, played a double game and tended to play off Cavour against Garibaldi. He gave Garibaldi covert support throughout his campaign, and the fact that Garibaldi admired the King (he related to his simplicity and coarse manners!) was crucial in bringing about unification. Garibaldi would never have handed over his conquests to Cavour as he did to the King, though we have noted the weakness of his situation in October 1860 (page 75). Victor Emmanuel was in fact much more shrewd than he has been given credit for, though his goal was entirely dynastic: the aggrandisement of Piedmont – the more territory, the better.

It seems that all the protagonists had a role to play in the final outcome, but it is true to say that only Garibaldi worked for unification. However, without Napoleon's war, Cavour's hard work and the symbolism of Victor Emmanuel's kingship, Garibaldi could not have achieved what he did achieve. Our close examination of the years 1858, 1859 and 1860 does highlight the role accident can play in history. Italian unification does seem to have come about more by accident then design, though we cannot discount the aspirations and drive for independence of the patriots. Admittedly they were small in number – the volunteers could be counted in tens of thousands, and the political activists were only a few thousand (in a population of over 25 million) – but without them, the Garibaldi episode cannot be fully explained, nor indeed can unification itself.

TASK

Discussion

The role of the main players plus Mazzini

Popular mythology made Mazzini 'the pen', Cavour 'the mind' and Garibaldi 'the sword' of unification. Napoleon III, whose role was crucial, was soon forgotten! And do not forget Victor Emmanuel. He was far from being a retiring, passive king, but the force of his personality varied from one moment to the next. He did not constantly strive for power – his aims were limited and he seems to come in and out of the story. Still, without him unification might not have taken place.

Appoint a student or a group of students to make the case for each of these protagonists. Although Mazzini did not play a role in the crucial events described in this chapter, he should be part of the debate as his reputation has grown with the passage of time, and he often commands an exam question in his own right. There is a brief biography in the Picture Gallery (page 9), but here follows an extended profile of him with more information:

Profile GUISEPPE MAZZINI 1805–72

Mazzini was born in Genoa and read law at Genoa University. Thereafter he became a 'poor man's lawyer', joined the Carbonari and was arrested in 1830. In 1831 he founded Young Italy ('Young' because members had to be under 40), a movement devoted to the formation of a united Italian Republic. It was at this time that he met and converted Garibaldi.

However, the failure of insurrections in the 1830s destroyed the movement (though its spirit lived on) and Mazzini went to live in London in 1837. In 1840 he revived Young Italy with little success. In 1848 he went to Milan, but his opposition to union with Piedmont made him unpopular there and he returned to England.

His greatest success came a year later in 1849 when he went to Rome and was elected a triumvir (one of three men to rule the city) and effective head of the government – but not for long as the Republic was soon crushed by the French army.

He returned to London and sponsored a number of unsuccessful conspiracies in the 1850s, but they nevertheless kept the Italian problem in the limelight. Orsini was a protegé and his assassination attempt on Emperor Napoleon III had significant consequences.

He played no part in the Franco-Austrian war and no part in Garibaldi's expedition to Sicily (though his agents were active there). He went to Naples briefly, but returned to London when the united kingdom of Italy was proclaimed.

In 1870 he was arrested en route to Sicily to lead a republican rising, but was released and pardoned after the occupation of Rome. He died in Pisa in 1872, disillusioned and disappointed.

It is extremely difficult to assess the importance of Mazzini's influence. There is no doubt that he was a great publicist, but the great champion of Italy lived most of his life in exile and played no role in the actual unification. So what is his importance? The really complicating factor is his reputation after his death. 'Mazzini made Italy' wrote The Spectator *in its obituary of him in 1872.*

With the unification of Italy and the growth of nationalism, his doctrines seemed to triumph and he came to be hailed as some sort of prophet. Indeed, Lloyd George described the Treaty of Versailles, with its alleged commitment to the principle of national self determination, as 'Mazzini's vindication'.

But what was his influence prior to unification? Undoubtedly his affirmation of Italian nationalism in the 1830s was important and it reached quite a wide (literate) audience. His acceptance as a leader of the Roman Republic in 1849 is a measure of his reputation. However, the lessons of 1848–9 were that revolution and republicanism were not realistic solutions to the Italian problem.

In the 1850s his influence receded as many former supporters abandoned him and joined the (royalist) National Society, though the threat of conspiracy exerted constant pressure on the rulers of the Italian states and kept the Italian issue in the headlines.

TASK

Accordingly, we can say that his significance as a symbol was immense. His was a life of dedication and single-minded purpose. He was an effective propagandist but his influence over Garibaldi proved to be his most decisive legacy. Yet he was never content with what came to pass: he described the Italy that came into being as a 'living lie' and he abhorred the monarchy. Italy would not become a republic until 1946, nearly three-quarters of a century after his death.

WARNING!

The story of unification does not end in 1861 as many students' essays mistakenly do! You need to carry the story through to 1870, the purpose of the next chapter.

CHAPTER FIVE

WAS ITALY REALLY UNIFIED?

Objectives
◢ To understand the acquisition of Venetia and Rome
◢ To determine the problems thrown up by Piedmontese centralisation.

This question operates on at least two levels. It can mean, was Italy unified geographically? Given the absence of Rome and Venetia, the answer in 1861 was clearly 'no'. And it can mean, was Italy unified in a national sense, i.e. was there political, social, economic and cultural integration, or was the rest of Italy simply conquered by Piedmont and subjected to a ruthless 'Piedmontisation'? A look at the decade from 1861 to 1870 should provide some answers.

Geographical unification

Aspromonte
The Kingdom of Italy had been proclaimed in 1861 but unification remained incomplete. Even prior to the proclamation, Cavour had announced that the kingdom should eventually include Rome and Venetia, and he had begun (unsuccessful) negotiations with the Pope. Pius IX steadfastly refused to negotiate, refused to recognise or even refer to Italy and referred only to Piedmont. Rome was certainly the priority rather than Venetia and Cavour hoped to persuade Napoleon to remove his troops from that city. Venetia, on the other hand, was a lesser priority as its acquisition would undoubtedly mean war with Austria.

Garibaldi took it upon himself to march on Rome in 1862. Aided by the ambivalent position adopted by both the Prime Minister, Rattazzi, and the King, Garibaldi gathered 2,000–3,000 volunteers unhindered in Sicily and crossed over to the mainland. At this point in early August governmental collusion was revealed and both the King and his Prime Minister, fearing diplomatic repercussions, decided to stop the expedition. In any event, Garibaldi had not been able to regenerate the support he had achieved in 1860. He was stopped by the Piedmontese army at Aspromonte, wounded in the ankle and imprisoned for a short time. This was an embarrassing episode for all parties concerned and the government fell at the end of the year.

Two years later in 1864 the Prime Minister, Minghetti, was able, by means of the September Convention, to persuade Napoleon to evacuate his troops from Rome (over a period of two years) on the understanding that the capital of Italy would be moved from Turin, not to Rome, but to Florence. This seems to have convinced Napoleon that the new state had abandoned its designs on Rome. It had not, but surprisingly it was to be Venetia rather than Rome that was to be obtained first, in a rather unexpected and inglorious way.

Venetia

Venetia came to Italy courtesy of Prussia. Bismarck, the Minister President of Prussia, anticipated war with Austria and as early as August 1865 had made overtures to the government in Florence. A treaty was finally signed on 8 April 1866, whereby Italy would receive Venetia in return for aiding Prussia in its war with Vienna. In May Austria made a similar sort of offer in return for neutrality, but it was not considered trustworthy. The war turned out to be something of a military humiliation for the new kingdom as the Austrians defeated the Italians both on land and at sea. First, at the second battle of Custoza on 24 June, a small-scale defeat was followed by an ignominious retreat; then on 20 July at the battle of Lissa a larger Italian fleet was defeated by a smaller Austrian one. Fortunately for Italy, Moltke and the Prussian army had smashed the Austrians at the battle of Königgrätz at the beginning of July, and Venetia was handed over (via Napoleon III) in October. Not one Venetian city had risen during the war and few Venetians had flocked to Garibaldi's standard. Still, the Italians had tied down 75,000 Austrian troops and Victor Emmanuel was able to comment, somewhat ambiguously (as was his wont), that Italy was made but incomplete – a further reference to the missing city of Rome.

Rome

French troops finally left Rome in December 1866 in accordance with the September Convention and Garibaldi, once again encouraged by Rattazzi (Prime Minister again – see list on page 86), saw another opportunity. In the autumn of 1867 Garibaldi raised a volunteer force of about 4,000 and set out to march on Rome. Once again Rattazzi changed course and distanced himself from the action. Napoleon immediately sent a French army back to the Papal State and at Mentana, on 3 November, Garibaldi's forces were easily defeated by a much larger Franco-Papal force of about 9,000. Clearly Garibaldi was not destined to march on Rome; and yet the eternal city was occupied some three years later, once again courtesy of Prussia.

Prime Ministers of Italy after Cavour

Bettino Ricasoli	June 1861 – February 1862
Urbano Rattazzi	March 1862 – December 1862
Luigi Carlo Farini	December 1862 – March 1863
Marco Minghetti	March 1863 – September 1864
Alfonso Lamarmora	September 1864 – June 1866
Bettino Ricasoli	June 1866 – April 1867
Urbano Rattazzi	April 1867 – October 1867
Luigi Frederico Menebrea	October 1867 – November 1869
Giovanni Lanza	December 1869 – July 1873

This was to be another, if not inglorious episode, then at least an anti-climactic one. Italy had been too weak financially to take advantage of deteriorating Franco-Prussian relations, and when war broke out between the two in July 1870, the government in Florence declared neutrality. In August, Napoleon withdrew his troops from Rome and only at that time did Victor Emmanuel begin to make some cautious military preparations. However, it was not until 2 September, when the battle of Sedan saw the defeat of France, the capture of the Emperor and the collapse of the Empire, that the King could consider taking unilateral action. Still the Pope would not negotiate, and on 11 September 50,000 Italian troops crossed the border into the Patrimony of St Peter. Pius IX only had about 15,000 troops at his disposal, but he believed in miracles! However, a miracle was not at hand and once the walls of Rome had been breached (20 September) he gave up in order to minimise the bloodshed (which was restricted to only 40 Italian and 19 Papal dead).

Entering Rome on the heels of the departing French was not exactly a glorious finale to the unification process. In keeping with the mood of anticlimax, when Victor Emmanuel made his formal entrance on 7 December, he was heard to utter the immortal words, 'At last we are here!' Rome immediately became the new capital, but the Pope refused to recognise the kingdom and continued to rail against 'Piedmontese treachery'. The Law of Papal Guarantees (May 1871) calmed the apprehensions of the international community by granting the Pope his diplomatic and spiritual independence within the Vatican (a 49-hectare enclave within the city of Rome). However, Pius refused to accept the pension offered him, excommunicated Victor Emmanuel and his government and declared himself to be 'the prisoner of the Vatican'. With this acquisition Italy became a reality (see Figure 6), but reconciliation with the Church was not formally reached until 1929.

National unification

In an oft-quoted statement, d'Azeglio is supposed to have said in 1861, 'Italy is made, now we must make Italians.' He had a point; after all, Italy had been conquered by Piedmont, it had not come about as a result of a great national movement. The vast mass of the population had little or no sense of belonging to a 'nation'. Indeed, many Italians had fought against Piedmont for Austria in 1859 and for Naples and the Pope in 1860. The people of Italy did not share a common language; only 2.5 per cent spoke Italian (most spoke dialects). Moreover, they were divided by fierce ancestral rivalries and there was an economic mismatch between the component parts, especially between north and south.

Cavour had originally favoured a certain amount of regional autonomy and this was certainly on offer at the time of the plebiscites. However, he soon came to change his mind. Referring to the south, he stated in December 1860, 'If riots break out ... we must impose national unification on the weakest and most corrupt part of Italy.' He lived long enough to see the start of the American Civil War and he did not want Italy to disintegrate in the same fashion. Moreover, after his death many felt Italy might well fall apart. Napoleon himself stated, 'The driver has fallen from the box: now we must see if the horses will bolt or go back to the stable.' Already prior to Cavour's death the south was slipping into civil war.

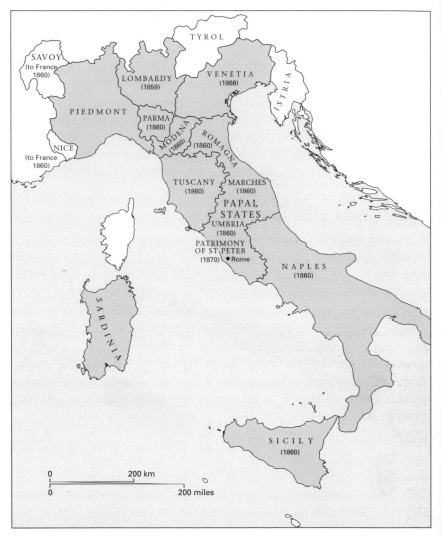

Figure 6 Italy in 1870

The Brigands' War

This is rather an inappropriate term for what was in fact a savage civil war in both Sicily and continental Naples. Moreover, the threat this posed to the existence of the new state cannot be underestimated. Beginning at the end of 1860, it was not contained until the end of

1866, and for much of the time it tied down more than 100,000 Italian soldiers. More Italians are believed to have died in this fighting (in excess of 16,000) than in all the fighting of 1848–9 and 1859–61 combined. The war is difficult to characterise – there were spontaneous peasant movements (the peasants were disappointed at the lack of land reforms and were crushed by economic hardship created by high taxation and free trade); there was a reaction in favour of the Bourbons and the Church directed by a sprinkling of supporters of the old regime; and there was a strange alliance of genuine brigands, disbanded soldiers and deserting conscripts, who were not hindered by the local elite because it was also totally disaffected (it had been excluded from the top jobs by northern appointees). However, the unrest turned out to be a golden opportunity for the new state to extend northern control over the south by brute force. Mass executions, troops and more troops were the response rather than any constructive policy, though in the long run the new state did not succeed in establishing a new power structure in this part of the kingdom.

Piedmontisation

Piedmont had conquered Italy; it is therefore hardly surprising that its institutions were imposed on the peninsula. Historians are agreed on this point. Denis Mack Smith stated that the speed of unification 'compelled ministers to treat the nation as an extension of Piedmont', and Harry Hearder stated, 'This part of the process of integration was undeniably one of "Piedmontisation".' Unification, after all, had come about in a sudden and unexpected way. There was no time to discuss or debate alternative approaches, and although rigid centralisation was ill-suited to a country with such ancient divisions in traditions and customs, the Piedmontese saw no alternative if Italy was to be prevented from falling apart. And it must be recognised that Cavour's undistinguished successors did at least manage to do that, though d'Azeglio wrote in 1863, 'Never was Italy as divided as she is now.'

Already prior to Cavour's death, the *Statuto*, the Piedmontese constitution, had been simply extended to all Italy. Thus only 2 per cent of the population had the vote and the ruling elite made no attempt to harness the political conservatism of the peasantry for the regime (as Napoleon was able to do so successfully in the Second Empire). The manipulation of elections in Piedmont was now applied to the whole peninsula; no parties emerged, only shaky coalitions which did not confront problems, but simply aimed at staying in office. The ruling party believed the state had to be centralised and given common institutions for it to survive. Thus the Piedmontese model of strong central government and weak local government was applied throughout the peninsula. The localities were controlled by prefects and sub-prefects in the provinces and mayors in the towns, who were all now royal appointees. Cavour needed these representatives to manipulate elections. A degree of autonomy in the localities that took account of local aspirations and traditions (i.e. decentralisation) could have spelt political suicide for some of the elite and would certainly have weakened its hold. Political and administrative centralisation was politically necessary, though it would prove to be problematic.

Ultimately, given the narrowness of the franchise, central government in the south and elsewhere was underpinned by coercive power rather than by the consent of the governed.

◢ Source

The remoteness of the state from civil society remained the most significant characteristic of united Italy ... Although it would be a distortion to ascribe all subsequent problems of the country solely to the hasty and exclusively political manner in which Italy was unified, the incapacity of the small ruling class to attract to its own values broad sectors of the population was a fundamental problem.

S. J. Woolf, **A History of Italy 1700–1860** (Methuen, 1979)

A representative of the Swiss government wrote as early as 4 June 1861, 'It is a misfortune for this country that the Piedmontese are hardly regarded by the others as being real Italians and in general show little interest in being considered as such, especially now that they have come into contact with Neapolitans and Sicilians whose customs and culture are so different from those in northern Italy.' It is interesting to remind ourselves again that Victor Emmanuel styled himself 'The Second' (his Piedmontese designation), and Italy's first parliament was in fact called the eighth Sardinian parliament.

The legal system was also unified and imposed on all (except in

Tuscany). The Civil Code was finally adopted in 1865. Piedmont's religious laws formally separated Church and state and inspired the Pope to issue a decree (1868) forbidding all Catholics to participate in the political life of the new state. In addition, common weights and measures and currency were applied and internal tariff barriers were removed. However, the application of liberal economics in the form of free trade proved damaging to the southern economy – to protected industry in particular. A unified Italian army was created, though disaffection was generated by the favour shown to Neapolitan officers over Garibaldi's men. Education became a central state responsibility, and the foreign and diplomatic service was blatantly Piedmontese, though few argued against this. Indeed, many of these measures were enlightened and sensible but the imposition of what was, for many, alien administrative and legal practices was not a happy experience.

Moreover, there was quite simply much more government than there had been before. The pressing needs of the military establishment led to the introduction of conscription which was very unpopular, and the desperate financial needs of the new kingdom led to the imposition of high taxes. Italians became the most heavily taxed people in Europe. The national debts of all the provinces were amalgamated and totalled some 2.5 billion lira in 1861. Two-thirds of the debt had been created by Piedmont's modernisation in the 1850s and by the loans taken out by the provisional regimes of 1859–61. In addition, military expenditure on the civil war of 1861–6 doubled the debt so that by 1869 interest payments alone took 60 per cent of the revenue, and the hated *grist tax* had to be reimposed. Sicily, for instance, had a debt that was only about a quarter of that of Piedmont, but now taxes went up 30 per cent to help pay for the national debt. Moreover, although Sicily represented 10 per cent of the Italian population, it only received about 3 per cent of expenditure. It is little wonder that unification was not embraced with wholehearted enthusiasm in this part of the kingdom. This brings us on to the most intractable problem faced by the new state: the gulf between north and south.

KEY TERM

Grist tax or *macinato* was a levy on the grinding of wheat which hit the poor particularly hard.

We have mentioned the civil war, the disastrous effects of free trade, conscription, higher taxes, and the imposition of alien administrative and legal practices. Few northern politicians understood the south, though d'Azeglio did suggest that the union of north and south was 'like going to bed with someone with smallpox'! There was a common misconception that the south was potentially rich but backward due to Bourbon misgovernment. It was felt that Naples only needed efficient government and 'Piedmontese morality' and everything would be all right. Still other Piedmontese believed Naples to be 'rotten', and Neapolitans to be 'barbarous, shiftless and lazy'. These were mistaken notions, and needless to say, this unsympathetic approach created more problems than it solved. Liberal politics could not easily be applied to an archaic social structure. In many ways the south was still a semi-feudal society. Eventually compromises had to be made, a network of corruption was established, and the government ended up ruling through the landowners. Thus in the south the new state found it easier to accept rather than destroy the local power structure.

Conclusion

In truth then the peninsula was Piedmontised – there was perhaps little alternative – and so it is possible to argue that Italy was never truly unified. Certainly the new kingdom did not solve the problems of the poverty-stricken south and there is still a north–south divide today. Cavour's original idea of just a northern Italian kingdom actually made a lot more sense. In this light, Garibaldi can be seen as a nuisance, hijacking Cavour's achievement and knocking it off course. But to suggest this might be a little perverse. Still, after the heady years of unification, the aftermath was certainly a disappointment. No wonder Mazzini stated in 1871, 'The Italy we represent today is a living lie.'

However, all this negativism overlooks the one, basic startling fact – Italy was unified and has remained unified ever since. This in itself has been a remarkable achievement. Maintaining unity has been a major job for subsequent politicians, while creating a sense of Italian national identity has been an even greater task. In this last matter the state has been aided and abetted by nationalist 'historians' whose distortions have served to create the myth of the *Risorgimento*. Thus it is to historiography that we now turn.

Essay

How important was foreign assistance in securing the unification of Italy by 1870?

This question clearly signposts the fact that the essay has to take in the episodes of 1866 and 1870, as well as those of 1859–61. But not all questions do (for example, *How much did outside influence affect the unification of Italy? How significant was the role of war and diplomacy in bringing about Italian unification?*). You have already been warned about this at the end of the previous chapter.

Remember, you should not confine yourself to discussing Napoleon, Cavour, Garibaldi and the events of 1859–61. The events of 1866 and 1870 and the contributions of Bismarck and Victor Emmanuel need to be discussed. Clearly, without Napoleon III and Bismarck, Italian unification might not have come about. In many ways the unification of Italy was inconceivable without outside influence. After all, prior to 1859 Italy consisted of a number of weak states which were controlled by outside influence (Austria). In this way any changes in Italy's status could only come about by a change in 'outside influence'. Indeed, the performance of the Italian forces in 1866 demonstrated quite clearly how limited were Italy's abilities to determine her own destiny.

All of these questions require you to focus on the role of foreign involvement, but you should not discount the Italian contribution either.

Suggested format

1 Introduction – address the question and state your position.
2 The international context – Austrian isolation and Napoleon III's ambitions 1856–9, his wish to eliminate Austrian influence and substitute that of France.
3 Napoleon's contribution and compromise 1859–60 – breaking Austrian control, creating a vacuum and making a deal; the role of Cavour.
4 Garibaldi steps into the vacuum but Cavour's reactions are very much dictated by his appreciation of the international context. He embraces unification with Napoleon's approval.
5 Venetia 1866 courtesy of Prussia – a less than glorious episode.
6 Rome 1870 – see pages 85–7.
7 Conclusion.

CHAPTER SIX

THE HISTORIOGRAPHY OF THE *RISORGIMENTO*

Objectives
⊿ To understand the development of the idea of the *Risorgimento*
⊿ To determine how far the concept has been undermined by recent historiography.

Introduction

This book has taken the view that the unification of Italy happened very suddenly and unexpectedly, almost accidentally, and was largely the result of war and diplomacy. Until recently, most Italians and Italian historians, however, saw unification very differently. To them it was the result of, or a stage in, their national revival, or *Risorgimento*. Unification was the culmination of a long-term evolutionary process undertaken by patriotic Italians. As a 1956 history of modern Italy put it, 'In common usage the word *Risorgimento* refers to the movement which led to the formation of the Italian national unitary state' (Giorgio Candeloro). Unification, then, was shown to be part of an unfolding grand design.

It is the purpose of this chapter to show how it was that Italian historians, in their efforts to create a greater (or at least some) sense of national feeling, were somewhat economical with the truth. In short, they tried to demonstrate that unification was the result of years of patriotic struggle in the face of Austrian oppression. While this might have had some political justification in the early years of the country's history in order to create a sense of common national identity (it reflected a realisation that there was in fact very little nationalism in the peninsula), it could not continue to be justified into the twentieth century. And yet it has had a long life, and it is only recently that we have been able to peel away the layers of myth and get closer to the truth, and appreciate what really happened.

◢ Source

Since unification historians and publicists have glorified all who have taken part in it . . .
Differences among Italians have been played down, the role of Italian soldiers
magnified, and the origins of the development pushed further and further back in time.
No doubt some such campaign was necessary to the strengthening of Italian feelings
of nationhood.

D. E. D. Beales, **The Risorgimento and the Unification of Italy** *(Longman, 1981)*

This last point reflects what d'Azeglio is alleged to have said in 1861
(see page 87) and for this reason, the past has come to have a
heightened political importance in Italy. After all, if the story of the
Risorgimento is false, then perhaps the existence of the unified Italian
state is not really justified at all.

The evolutionary Italocentric approach is also reflected – with slight
regional bias – in the various *Risorgimento* museums in Italian cities, for
example in Turin (where Charles Albert is the hero), Genoa (in
Mazzini's family home), Venice (where Manin looms large) and Milan.
The National Museum of the Risorgimento housed in the basement of
the Victor Emmanuel Monument in Rome (see Figure 7) has been
closed for several years, but its layout is instructive. The first room
deals with the 1780s and subsequent rooms carry the story forward and
get larger. There is a huge room for 1848 and that for 1859 to 1861 is
enormous. Thereafter the rooms get smaller. The message conveyed is
loud and clear: unification was an inevitable historical process, and
further, it was a process carried out by Italians themselves.

The nineteenth century

Now it is inevitable in some ways that the victors write the history and
it is not surprising that this was the case with Italy. Thus the moderates
– Cavour and Victor Emmanuel – were praised at the expense of the
radicals – Mazzini and Garibaldi. The dynastic historians of the late
nineteenth century fabricated a *Risorgimento* in which the House of
Savoy had been the standard bearer of liberal constitutionalism,
allying itself with whatever progressive forces were to hand for the
greater good of the Italian people. However, this was easily subjected to

Figure 7 The Victor Emmanuel Monument in Rome

criticism and the shortcomings of the monarchs were soon exposed. In any event, this approach was not the main theme of early historiography. Most nineteenth-century Italian history was written by sympathisers of Cavour. His glorification transformed him from a statesman who could profit brilliantly from his errors, into the perfect manipulator of European diplomacy who unified Italy according to a predetermined plan. To be fair, Luigi Zini, who was perhaps the first historian to analyse Cavour (in a four-volume work published in 1866), was aware of his shortcomings and recognised that Cavour only embraced the idea of Italian unification very late in the day, but Zini was an exception.

Less critical and more influential – it was still regarded as a standard text in the 1950s – was Nicomede Bianchi's eight volumes of diplomatic documents with commentary, the *Storia documentata della diplomazia europea in Italia dell'anno 1814 all 'anno 1861*, published from 1865 to 1872. According to Bianchi, Cavour's genius was the main factor in the unification of Italy. Luigi Chiala continued in this vein in his six-volume edition of Cavour's letters (1884–7) playing down the radicals and making Cavour the central and most successful figure. Another historian, Giuseppe Massari, was extravagant in his praise for both

Cavour and Victor Emmanuel, but his biographies (1875 and 1878) were more fiction than history and contain much invented dialogue. Nevertheless, they have been influential.

As the decades passed the weaknesses and problems that emerged in the new state were contrasted with an increasingly uncritical and complacent vision of the triumphs that led to unification. Moreover, this tendency extended to the other famous actors of the *Risorgimento* as well, so that instead of being considered as persons with opposing ideologies, they became collaborators. As we have mentioned before (page 81), popular mythology made Mazzini 'the pen', Cavour 'the mind' and Garibaldi 'the sword' of unification.

Carolo Tivaroni, in his nine-volume work *Storia critica del risorgimento* published between 1888 and 1897, maintained that the work of Mazzini, Garibaldi and Cavour was all necessary for Italian unification.

◢ Source

In this lies the greatness of the unitarians, and of Mazzini more than anyone: that they maintained intact their faith in unity, when it appeared to be madness to everyone who considered himself wise. Here lies the glory of Mazzini and Garibaldi: that they constrained the House of Savoy to accept unity. Without doubt however, if the king had made a premature proclamation of unity [in 1859], when Mazzini wanted him to do so, it would have turned all the other Italian princes into open enemies; instead of remaining neutral they would have sent their armies to help Austria. So the prudence of Cavour and Vittorio Emanuele played their part, just as did the constancy of Mazzini and the audacity of Garibaldi. Without these four men, each one in his own sphere of action, what would have happened to Italy if any one of them had been lacking? How, with only Mazzini, or with only Garibaldi, could Austria ever have been defeated? And how, with only Cavour and with only Vittorio Emanuele could anyone have thought of overcoming the grave obstacles presented by Rome and Naples? And without Naples and Rome would the Kingdom of Italy not have remained always under the tutelage of France?

C. Tivaroni, **Storia critica del risorgimento**, vol. IX

Francesco De Sanctis, the great literary scholar and contemporary of Cavour, went further; for him it was not simply a matter of elements complementing each other, it was a matter of cooperation: 'Italy was fortunate in that the genius of Cavour and the patriotism of Garibaldi worked together.' Another influential work was Alfredo Oriani's *La lotta politica in Italia*, published in 1892, which painted the *Risorgimento* in vivid colours: 'no modern hero was the equal of Garibaldi; no apostle of politics had a soul more tragic than Mazzini, words more evocative, a patience more unconquered', and 'Cavour's [idea] was a vortex which attracted, encircled, condensed and formed a fatherland'.

Oriani actually made his biggest impact after the First World War, appealing to both liberals and Fascists. Non-Italian historians did not wax quite so lyrical, though many were liberal and nationalist and showed a tendency, similar to Italian historiography of the same period, to see the whole history of Italy in the nineteenth century as a romantic epic leading to unification. The most famous was G. M. Trevelyan whose trilogy on Garibaldi appeared between 1907 and 1911. He wrote:

◢ Source

Nothing is more remarkable – though to believers in nationality and ordered liberty nothing is more natural – than the stability of the Italian kingdom ... The foundations of human liberty and social order exist there on a firm basis. The growing difficulties of the social problem, common to all Europe, find at least mitigation in the free political institutions of a nation so recently created by the common effort of all classes ... In Italy the traditions of the Risorgimento unite and elevate her children. All classes from the king to the workman, all provinces from Piedmont to Sicily are bound together by these memories of a history so recent yet so poetical and so profound.

G. M. Trevelyan, **Garibaldi and the Making of Italy**, (Longman, 1911)

The twentieth century

In the twentieth century matters have become more complicated. **Fascism** tried to claim the glory of unification for itself; Roman Catholics, their church reconciled at last with the new kingdom in 1929, began to exalt those of their adherents who had sympathised with the national movement; and socialists both emphasised and reinterpreted the whole story in terms of their theories of history.

KEY TERM

Fascism is a system of extreme right-wing dictatorship, but in origin it refers to the political movement founded by Benito Mussolini in Italy in 1919.

Criticism of the parliamentary system and the policies of the new state did lead to criticisms of the way Italy had been unified and these were exploited by the Fascists. Fascist historiography sought to highlight the elements of power and national grandeur whilst underplaying the theme of liberty. For Fascists the hero was Garibaldi, rather than Cavour the parliamentarian. Thus the story was a success until 1861 when everything went wrong – Italy became a liberal parliamentary state! Gioacchino Volpe described Fascism as a conscious revival of the true *Risorgimento* that had died in 1861, but this time with the participation of the people. He maintained that the first phase had created the Italian state, and it was to be the role of Fascism in the second phase to create the Italian nation.

Against this background of the collapse of Liberal Italy in the 1920s, the philosopher Benedetto Croce (1866–1952) rose to the *Risorgimento's* defence, emphasising the progress that had been made since unification and arguing that Italian unification was the 'masterpiece' of European liberalism. He was certainly prone to exaggeration, but opponents of Fascism understood the historical context of his interpretation. In his view it was the war that destroyed Liberal Italy; he saw no link with Fascism which he viewed as an aberration.

After the Second World War, however, Marxist historians criticised Croce. The Marxist 'school' condemned the *Risorgimento* for uniting Italy with little popular participation. The impetus for this criticism was provided by Antonio Gramsci (1891–1937) in his prison note-books. He interpreted the *Risorgimento* as a missed opportunity. He believed the moderates had denied the radicals a fair share of an achievement to which both parties had contributed. The privileged classes had looked after themselves. In Gramsci's view Cavour 'conceived unity as an increasing of the Piedmontese state and of the patrimony of the dynasty, not at base a national movement, but a royal conquest'. The failure to mobilise the popular movement caused a breach between state and society which led to political instability and social disorder – all of which led directly to Fascism. The effect of Gramsci's challenge to Croce was to polarise *Risorgimento* historiography, with liberals on one side, and socialists on the other. However, it was to be a British historian, Denis Mack Smith (b. 1920), who gave a new twist to *Risorgimento* history and proved to be most influential, in Italy as well as in the English-speaking world.

When he published his *Cavour and Garibaldi 1860* in 1954, it created a considerable stir in Italy. Mack Smith emphasised the fact that unification resulted from bitter struggles between Italians, and even disputes and uncertainties between patriots, divisions which had been hidden from scholars by inaccessible or doctored material. As he himself put it:

◢ Source

Such falsification of history was excusable in the early years after 1860 when there was an urgent need to consolidate the not very vigorous sense of national unity ... But the excuse of political emergency became less valid in the course of time. Early in the twentieth century, when the argument was advanced that such concealment had become harmful and even dangerous by obscuring any truthful understanding of some fundamental national problems, Prime Minister Giovanni Giolitti made the discouragingly negative reply that 'it would not be right to let beautiful legends be discredited by historical criticism'.

D. Mack Smith, **Cavour and Garibaldi**, (CUP, 1954) taken
from the introduction to the second edition, 1985

Mack Smith went on to question the whole notion of the *Risorgimento* by emphasising the role of accident and also the crucial role played by the Great Powers. In addition, he showed that most of those involved were not aiming at unification at all. This was not well received in Italy where one reviewer wrote (in 1960) that Mack Smith had reduced the *Risorgimento* to a development brought about 'through fortunate circumstances, to selfish interests, to a complex of material needs, to strokes of fortune and diplomatic deceits ... he takes away its soul'. However, his views, based on considerable research and a mastering of the documentation, have been widely accepted by British and

American historians. Of course not everyone has accepted that there was so little nationalism in Italy and not everyone has accepted the notion that Italian unification was wholly accidental, but his views have largely prevailed and continue to carry weight.

One effect of this more realistic approach to nineteenth-century Italian history had been to release it from the stranglehold that unification had on it and allow a new generation of historians to switch focus to other aspects of Italian history: social change, the family, cultural change, regionalism, even the governments of preunification (Restoration) Italy, aspects which had hitherto been largely ignored. These developments can only further enrich our understanding of what was, and is, and will continue to be, a controversial subject. We are probably much closer now to a realistic reconstruction of what actually happened, but also much more aware of the complexity involved in arriving at an agreed set of explanations.

Notemaking on the historiography of the *Risorgimento*

Usually the headings and subheadings of the chapters provide the basic framework for notemaking, but in this case using the names of the historians is probably the best approach:

1 Introduction

2 Nineteenth century
  a Zini
  b Bianchi
  c Chiala
  d Massari
  e Tivaroni
  f De Sanctis
  g Oriani
  h Trevelyan

3 Twentieth century
  a Volpe
  b Croce
  c Gramsci
  d Mack Smith

CHAPTER SEVEN

POSTSCRIPT: ITALY SINCE UNIFICATION – DISILLUSION AND DEVELOPMENT

Objectives

◢ To consider the disappointments and difficulties after unification
◢ To understand the growing north–south divide
◢ To understand Italy's political instability
◢ To briefly bring the story down to the present day.

Disillusion with the new state soon set in. Italy did not become a great power as many expected it would, and the 'age of poetry' was followed by the 'age of prose'. Garibaldi wrote in 1880 two years before his death: 'It was a very different Italy which I spent my life dreaming of; not the impoverished and humiliated country which we now see ruled by the dregs of the nation.' Garibaldi was not alone in this disillusion: millions emigrated. Why was this? We have already touched upon a number of the reasons in chapters 5 and 6.

For one thing, Italy had not been created by popular participation (the plebiscites had been largely rigged) and there was no real attempt to develop the state on a popular basis. For instance, no concession was made to regional autonomy despite the varying traditions of the different parts of Italy. Ferrari, a Piedmontese member of parliament, criticised this outlook at the time of unification in October 1860: 'The general idea was to say to the other parts of Italy – revolt for your grievances against your rulers is justified; but after the insurrection there must be no discussion: you must become Piedmontese.' He went on to state how unsatisfactory and unfair this was and to advocate a federal system, but his arguments were rejected.

As we have seen, government was imposed upon the people by a narrow elite, and the Piedmontese constitution, the *Statuto*, was extended over the whole peninsula. The 2.5 per cent electorate was urban and propertied whereas the bulk of the people were landless peasantry; this was not a recipe for stability. Moreover, the system was corrupt and unstable: there were 67 ministries in the 74 years between the creation of the *Statuto* (1848) and Mussolini (1922), and of course the weak coalitions did not face up to Italy's real problems. This also gave the King plenty of scope for interference. It would perhaps be unrealistic to expect full democracy in the nineteenth century; the electorate was extended to 7 per cent in 1882. However, the political system was divisive, leaving out republicans and, more significantly, Catholics. Given the fact that the bulk of the population were practising Catholics the quarrel with the Pope was unfortunate to say the least. However, the Pope himself was irreconcilable, and it was not until Mussolini that this problem was resolved.

The most intractable problem remained the north–south divide. The south was poor; it needed help. However, as we have seen, northern politicians did not see it that way, believing poverty to be the result of laziness and corruption. The other real problem, though, was that government authority in the south was quite weak, and had to be established by means of continuing the cycle of corruption through the landowners. As we have already observed, the new state found it easier to accept than to destroy the local power structure. In fact, the southern elite became much more powerful after unification since it was able to manipulate the parliamentary system and benefit from government policy. For instance, when the government sold off Church lands in Sicily (which covered about one-tenth of the island), the opportunity for a fair redistribution was lost as they were snapped up by just a few families. A survey taken in Sicily between 1907 and 1910 showed that 50 per cent of the land was owned by just 0.1 per cent of the population.

Moreover, as we have already indicated, because of unification the rest of Italy was saddled with a huge debt and resulting high taxation. Northern Italy did not do too badly out of this, but the table below shows that the people south of Florence bore an unfair burden.

Area	Proportion of wealth	Proportion of tax burden
Northern Italy	48%	40%
Central Italy	25%	35%
Southern Italy	27%	32%

But Italy was in any case economically weak: it possessed no coal or iron ore reserves – significant deficiencies in the industrial era – and it never came to play a leading role among the Great Powers; it was in fact the least of the Great Powers. However, welding 27 million disparate people together was a huge task and we might reflect that given the enormous problems Italy faced, it has done well to survive and prosper. It would be instructive to finish by briefly surveying Italian history since unification.

Liberal Italy

The new Italy failed to deliver economic benefits and did not defuse tensions. The moderate right-wing coalition (*destra storica*) that ruled after Cavour was mainly concerned to balance the budget. Consequently, between 1862 and 1880 taxation doubled and the standard of living of the mass of the people fell from an already low level. In addition, free trade killed off protected industries in the south and depressed its inefficient agriculture. All this led to social unrest. In the absence of a benign Church presence because of the ongoing quarrel with the Pope, order could only be maintained by coercion and support for the existing social structure. However, in the case of the south the existing social structure perpetuated economic backwardness by preventing the move from farm to factory.

The moderate right was replaced in 1876 by the moderate left (*sinistra storica*), but little changed. Although there were 22 ministries between the occupation of Rome (1870) and the outbreak of the First World War (1915 for Italy), politics were dominated by three men: Agostino Depretis between 1876 and 1887, Francesco Crispi between 1887 and 1896, and Giovanni Giolitti between 1903 and 1914. In fact it was Depretis who in 1882 coined the expression '***transformism***' by stating, 'If anyone wishes to transform himself and become progressive ... can I reject him?' By this means the opposition was absorbed and the right wing 'transformed'. The *sinistra storica* monopolised political power thereafter.

KEY TERM

Transformism was the system whereby the government assured itself of a majority in parliament either by a preliminary deal with leaders of the opposition who were then absorbed into the government as ministers, or by granting favours to deputies in return for support, or by combining both methods.

We have already pointed out that Italy's economy was weak, disadvantaged by lack of resources and accumulated debts, and that free trade also hurt native industry and agriculture. It was principally cheap grain from the USA and Russia that caused real problems in the 1870s and 1880s. Crispi, who succeeded Depretis, was committed to a policy of protection which over 30 years was beneficial (though it protected inefficient southern agriculture). However, in the short term, tariff wars (with France in particular) had damaging effects and led to unrest and uprisings.

Crispi fell from power in 1896, not because of economic problems but because of Italy's failure to occupy Abyssinia and because of her humiliating defeat at Adowa (a humiliation that was only partially offset by Giolitti's conquest of Libya and the Dodecanese in 1911–12).

The economic downturn at the end of the century led to quite a bit of turbulence – in 1898 nearly half the provinces were under martial law and in 1900 King Umberto I was assassinated. However, the corner had been turned and Italy finally experienced something of an industrial revolution. Between 1896 and 1914 industrial production doubled and national income rose by 50 per cent, aided by public works and military expenditure. However, industrialisation was confined to the north-western triangle of Turin, Milan and Genoa, and aided by the increased agricultural productivity of Lombardy, Piedmont and Emilia.

There was no take-off in the south and this northern industrial development had the effect of widening the gap between north and south still further. Although the government now spent a bit more on these depressed areas, it continued to operate through the southern landowners and their cronies. Indeed, Giolitti very much depended upon southern deputies whose method of election was blatantly corrupt. Increasingly the people of the south escaped poverty by emigration; it is estimated that something like eight million left between 1901 and 1913, bound mainly for the United States.

Whereas Crispi had concentrated on the economy but had ignored the social question, Giolitti sought to restore social peace by a series of reforms, in particular granting workers rights. Giolitti was successful and achieved a measure of stability. Moreover, in 1912 he dramatically extended the franchise from 3 million to 8.5 million. However, he fell from power in 1914 when his supporters discovered that he had made a deal with the Church to get *non expedit* (the papal ban on political participation) lifted in half the provinces. There had been a gradual healing process between Church and state since Pius IX's death in 1878, but secularisation was considered to be a fundamental legacy of the *Risorgimento* that could not be betrayed. In fact, Giolitti's move towards democracy weakened Liberal Italy and had the effect of creating greater polarisation rather than convergence, as extreme right-wing (nationalist) and left-wing (socialist) groups grew in importance. Polarisation was accentuated still further by the outbreak of war in Europe in August 1914 as politicians divided between those who wanted Italy in and those who wanted Italy out. Eventually Prime Minister Salandra took Italy in, on the side of Britain, France and Russia in May 1915, but the country was not prepared for war and it did not go well.

War and Fascism

Although Italy was allied to Germany and Austria in the Triple Alliance of 1882, which had been renewed and strengthened twice down to 1914, the kingdom had signed a neutrality pact with France in 1902 and enjoyed good relations with both Britain and Russia. When the European war broke out in 1914 there was not only a division between interventionists and neutralists, but also a division among the interventionists as to which side to be on. Austria was still seen as the traditional enemy and her expansion in the Balkans had caused considerable irritation. Moreover, it was territory from Austria that Italy principally wanted. The Prime Minister, Salandra, and the King favoured intervention on the Entente side (Britain, France and Russia) and went behind parliament's back to obtain the Treaty of London in

May 1915. In return for entering the war, this promised Italy not only Italian-speaking areas but the South Tyrol, Istria, half the Dalmatian coast and territory in Africa and the Middle East. Despite opposition to the war, parliament felt bound to honour this (most attractive) treaty.

Italy then went to war in May 1915 against Austria only. The war was an unmitigated disaster. Over the next two and a half years there were eleven offensives which gained about twenty kilometres at the expense of 200,000 dead. Moreover, this meagre advance was quickly lost by the defeat at the battle of Caporetto in October 1917. This German-inspired attack pushed 130 kilometres into Italy in three weeks, destroyed much of the Italian army and threatened to knock her out of the war. French and British divisions had to be rushed in to stabilise the front. At least the war now became a national one of defence. After a year's stalemate the Italians hit back and won the battle of Vittorio Veneto against an Austrian army that was already disintegrating. This restored some pride, but arguably Italy was not in as strong a position in 1919 as it had been in 1915. This gave rise to what came to be described as the 'mutilated victory'.

Basically Woodrow Wilson, the American President, would not endorse the Treaty of London. He favoured the creation of Yugoslavia and there was general indifference to Italian demands. Istria and Dalmatia were not forthcoming and Britain and France shared out the colonial mandates among themselves. This bred disillusion which was dramatically fuelled by the post-war recession. Price inflation, depressed wages, unemployment and strikes created economic and social chaos. The occupation of factories in 1920 seemed to point to a socialist revolution, though in truth the fear was exaggerated.

On top of all this a new electoral law in 1919 brought democracy (for men) and created proportional representation, which in turn created political chaos. The two largest parties, the socialist and the *Popolari* (the Catholic party), would not cooperate. Consequently the Liberal politicians gained a new lease of life but no majority. There were five prime ministers in three years. The largest party, the Socialists, would not participate in government at all (the communists broke away in 1921) and the *Popolari* would not cooperate with anti-clerical liberals. Into this vacuum stepped Benito Mussolini and the Fascist party.

Mussolini had begun as a socialist and when he started his Fascist movement in 1919, it too had been left wing. However, he rapidly moved to the right, became violently anti-socialist, gained the support of the Pope, the middle classes, the industrialists, the landowners and even peasant proprietors – indeed, all who feared a communist take-over and the destruction of private property. Mussolini even abandoned republicanism. Giolitti tried to 'transform' Fascism by bringing the party into his electoral bloc, but he only succeeded in getting them 35 seats in the Chamber and a taste for power.

The left played into Mussolini's hands by organising a general strike in July–August 1922 which the Fascists easily smashed. The road to power was now open. Mussolini threatened a violent coup (the 'March on Rome'), but he also negotiated and once the King was assured of his position, Mussolini was invited to form a government in October 1922.

Fascism did not become a mass movement until after the Fascists had obtained power, and Mussolini moved slowly and not very decisively over the next few years to consolidate his power. In fact, it was not until 1926 that the Liberal state was finally swept away and Italy became a one-party state. However, thereafter Mussolini was able to consolidate his position within the party, which after a decade had become essentially middle class. By the time he had signed the Lateran Accords with the Papacy in 1929, Mussolini had achieved unrivalled stability at home and a new respect abroad where he was admired for creating an alternative to socialism. However, his 'Corporate State', which was meant to promote class collaboration rather than class conflict, was operated very much in favour of the employer and the state.

Despite economic failures, contemporaries felt the Fascist state weathered the Depression well, and there is no doubt that the high levels of state intervention stimulated important modern industries, such as electricity, steel and chemicals. Of course in much of the Fascist regime, appearance took precedence over reality. Mussolini described his regime as totalitarian but it should be remembered that the monarchy remained intact, and the King was the commander-in-chief of all the armed forces. The Vatican proved something of a Trojan horse: the Church had considerable influence and was critical of the regime. Still, it is true to say that Mussolini had a great deal of control over foreign policy, but this is where he made most of his mistakes.

There was continuity in foreign policy in that Fascist Italy wished to adjust the balance of power in the Balkans, the Mediterranean and Africa, but innovation in the sense that policy was continuously expansionist and nationalistic. In the 1920s Mussolini was cautious either by necessity or design, but the rise of Hitler created more opportunities. Britain and France overestimated Italian power and wanted Mussolini's friendship. Mussolini hoped they would give him a free hand in Abyssinia. When they did not, he turned to Hitler.

Mussolini invaded Abyssinia in October 1935 and announced annexation to cheering crowds in May 1936. Although Abyssinia turned out to be an economic millstone, the condemnation of its acquisition by the international community had the perverse effect of creating considerable national solidarity; Mussolini was at the peak of his popularity. Unfortunately *Il Duce*, as he was known, was temperamentally unable to keep out of the limelight and he immediately got involved in the Spanish Civil War on a large scale, again with no return. He enjoyed another burst of popularity in 1938 when he arbitrated the peaceful Munich agreement, but his invasion of Albania (another worthless territory) and Pact of Steel with Hitler in 1939 brought only trepidation to a people who did not want to go to war. When war came in September 1939 Italy was not ready. Mussolini was forced to declare non-belligerence – to great popular relief – but when it looked as though the war was almost won, he could not stay out.

He declared war on Britain and France on 10 June 1940 hoping for easy gains, but the war was not over and there followed spectacular defeats in Greece, North Africa and East Africa. Hitler had to come to his rescue and by 1941 Italy had in effect become a German satellite. It was by now clear that after twenty years of Fascist rule loyalty to the movement was only skin deep. People had joined to further their careers; as soon as the regime got into trouble they jumped ship. Once Sicily was invaded by Anglo-American forces in July 1943, Mussolini was removed by his own party and the King took over. There followed a period of indecisiveness which involved deceiving the Germans and negotiating with the Allies. By the time Italy surrendered on 8 September, the Germans had managed to reinforce their army and they were able to rapidly occupy two-thirds of the peninsula.

Unfortunately this had the effect of creating another north–south divide, with the Allied occupation of the south reinforcing its dependency culture while the north spawned an organised resistance movement, largely dominated by socialists and communists, which threw up the leaders of the future. For the next nineteen months a difficult and slow campaign subjected the Italian people to all the horrors of war.

Initially the Resistance would not recognise the royal government, but perversely Stalin did so in March 1944, forcing the Allies and other Italians to do the same. After the occupation of Rome in June 1944, the United States gave the Italian coalition government power on the understanding that after the war Victor Emmanuel III would abdicate in favour of his son, the crown prince, Umberto, who became 'Lieutenant of the Realm'. The future of the monarchy would then be decided by the Italian people.

Mussolini, who had been rescued by a daring SS raid as early as 12 September 1943, had been set up in charge of a puppet German republic (of Salo) in the north of Italy. In April 1945 he was captured and executed by partisans and the German army finally surrendered. The war was over and hopes were high that a genuinely popular and democratic Italy could now be constructed.

The Republic

In the aftermath of the war, Italy became a democratic republic (women were given the vote too). Victor Emmanuel III abdicated in April 1946 in favour of his son, who became Umberto II, but he narrowly lost the referendum in June by 54 per cent to 46 per cent. The new constitution officially proclaimed on 1 January 1948 retained proportional representation and political life came to be polarised between the Communists on the left and the Christian Democrats on the right. The Christian Democrats were the largest party, enjoying much of their support among the peasantry and in the south; they were the heirs to the *Popolari*. In the first elections they polled 34 per cent whereas the Liberal party all but disappeared (7 per cent). The combined left-wing vote – 39 per cent split between the Socialists (20 per cent) and the Communists (19 per cent) – reflected the legacy of the Resistance. Both left-wing parties were committed to the parliamentary system, but this was the beginning of the Cold War and the United States did not wish to see a left-wing government in place. In 1947 the Socialists split, which explains why the Communists became the second party in Italy, an unusual occurrence for western Europe.

In 1948 the Christian Democrats polled 48 per cent of the vote and the left 31 per cent (the Socialists were down to 10 per cent) and this polarisation was to be a permanent feature of post-war Italian politics – as indeed it had been just after the First World War. Given the Cold War situation, Italy virtually became a one-party state – there was no alternation of power since, as we have noted, the United States would never allow the Communists a share in government. However, over time the Christian Democrats lost votes and had to make frequent deals with small parties. This made politics more and more unstable. Moreover, the Christian Democrats abused their monopoly of power and sought to maximise their control of central and local administration for the benefit of themselves and their friends. Their reliance on popular support in the south also ensured that they were entwined in a web of corruption.

Thus the Republic did not turn out to be the new society envisaged by the Resistance, but a democratic framework with civil rights had been established and given the circumstances of 1945, this was quite an achievement. The incomprehensible paradox to outsiders of course was the fact that Italy managed to combine this political chaos with something of an 'economic miracle'. The basis for Italy's economic recovery was US aid – 1.75 billion dollars between 1943 and 1947 (and the Marshal Plan thereafter to 1952) – but the republic also benefited from the low lira, low labour costs and trade liberalisation.

Italy joined NATO in 1949 and the European Union in all its many guises. The index of industrial production doubled between 1953 and 1961 and GDP went up 6.5 per cent per annum between 1958 and

1963. However, the north–south divide remained and got worse, as the south grew at only half the rate of the north. In excess of five million southerners moved to the north to work in industry there. Continuing poor economic conditions enabled crime and corruption to continue to flourish. Vast sums of money were spent on the south but much of it 'disappeared'. Organised crime (mainly by the Mafia) financed parties which in turn procured more funds to keep the process going. People in the north resented paying tax which went to criminals. Still, by the 1990s the north enjoyed 79 per cent of the country's purchasing power, whereas the south, with 35 per cent of the population, only possessed 21 per cent. The north–south divide remains. However, the growth rate, which averaged over 5 per cent per annum between 1950 and 1980 and continued into the 1980s with the development of a sophisticated consumer society (in the north at least), propelled Italy into the premier league of the world's economic powers.

However, there were some real underlying problems. Public services were inefficient and the black economy was more widespread in Italy than in other countries. The huge public debt – created by funding the south – had by the 1990s exceeded GDP. Politically things went from bad to worse. Social and political violence had always been part of Italian life as indeed had organised crime (the Mafia spread into the north in the post-war period), but from 1969 there was added the dimension of terrorism which peaked in 1978 with the assassination of Prime Minister Moro. Thereafter it gradually subsided.

The Christian Democrat vote continued to fall; in 1975 it fell as low as 34 per cent with the Communists just 1 per cent behind. A National Solidarity Coalition with Communist support came together briefly to fight terrorism in the late 1970s, but the polarisation remained. Since the 1960s the Christian Democrats had been able to recruit Socialist support at different times. In the 1980s it was to be a Socialist, Bettino Craxi, who dominated politics both by his ability and by traditional wheeling and dealing. However, with the collapse of the Soviet Union in 1991 the Italian people saw no reason to put up any longer with the old corrupt system. After all, a Soviet take-over (via a Communist electoral victory) was no longer the only alternative. The elections in 1992 produced a political upheaval as the old parties lost ground and the *Lega del Nord* – a movement which harked back to a populist version of federalism – polled 9 per cent. In the same year a corruption scandal assumed incredible dimensions as it implicated all those in high places, including Craxi and other former prime ministers. Confidence in parliament evaporated and in local elections in 1993 the Socialist and Christian Democrat votes collapsed. In the same year the proportional representation system was drastically modified. The Christian Democrats dissolved themselves (but reformed as the *Popolari*), as did the Socialists in 1994.

In 1994 the media tycoon, Silvio Berlusconi, came from nowhere to capture power and the traditional parties disappeared altogether. He too has since gone, also accused of corruption. *Plus ça change, plus c'est la même chose* (the more things change, the more they stay the same) and so it goes on. Italian politics were a mess (55 governments between 1945 and 1998), but the economy made the criteria for the single currency – a miracle that would have no doubt even impressed Pius IX.

It would be foolish to try and predict the future. In the light of the upheavals of the 1990s many commentators have suggested that the unification of Italy was a colossal mistake and that Italy might break up under the pressure of federalism. However, what is true is that the work of Cavour and Garibaldi has survived so many crises – defeat in war, political polarisation, economic hardship, the north–south divide, corruption, governmental instability, etc. – and we should not be surprised to see it survive the present one as well. Indeed, without a crisis Italy would just not be Italy.

FURTHER READING

This is a short, selective bibliography featuring works longer than this one. Many of the books cited have extensive bibliographies.

Collections of documents

D. Beales *The Risorgimento and the Unification of Italy* (Longman edition, 1981) – features a very full introduction and useful, full documentary extracts.

V. Brendon *The Making of Modern Italy 1800–71*, (Hodder & Stoughton, 1998) – recent, concise and affordable.

D. Mack Smith *The Making of Italy 1796–1870* (Macmillan edition, 1988) – features a large number of documentary extracts.

General histories

R. Absalom *Italy since 1800* (Longman, 1995) – a thought-provoking survey.

J. A. Davis *Conflict and Control* (Humanities Press, 1988) – mainly about law and order but has wider implications.

S. P. Di Scala *Italy: From Revolution to Republic* (Westview Press, 1995) – very sympathetic to Italian achievements.

J. A. S. Grenville *Europe Reshaped 1848–1878* (Fontana, 1976) – Chapter 12 deals with the Unification of Italy.

H. Hearder *Italy in the Age of the Risorgimento 1790–1870* (Longman, 1983) – a useful survey with a number of potted biographies.

S. Woolf *A History of Italy 1700–1860* (Methuen, 1979) – focuses on Italian society.

Biographies

H. Hearder *Cavour* (Longman, 1994) – a sympathetic survey.

E. E. Y. Hales *Pio Nono* (Eyre and Spottiswoode, 1956).

D. Mack Smith *Cavour* (Methuen, 1985) – less sympathetic.

D. Mack Smith *Garibaldi: A Portrait in Documents* (Rassigli Edition, 1982).

D. Mack Smith *Mazzini* (Yale, 1994).

J. F. McMillan *Napoleon III* (Longman, 1991).

J. Ridley *Garibaldi* (Constable, 1974).

The Risorgimento

F. J. Coppa *The Italian Wars of Independence* (Longman, 1992) – good on the international dimension.

L. Riall *The Italian Risorgimento* (Routledge, 1994) – a survey of recent research on the period 1815–60.

W. G. Shreeves *Nationmaking in Nineteenth-Century Europe* (Nelson, 1984) – very useful for generating discussion.

INDEX

KEY TERMS

Ancien Régime   14
Bourgeoisie   29
Devolution   76
Fascism   99
Grist Tax   91
Liberalism   21
Reactionary   20
Restoration   14
Statuto   38
Transformism   106

PROFILES

King Charles Albert   30
King Ferdinand II   32
Mazzini, Guiseppe   81–3
Metternich, Clemens von   22
Radetzky, Johann   36

MAPS

Italy in 1815   7
Italy after Villafranca (July 1859)   60
Italy after the annexation of the
   Duchies (March 1860)   62
Italy after Oct 1860   72
Italy in 1870   88

MAIN INDEX

Aspromonte   84
Austria   6, 16, 22, 33–5, 38, 47–50,
   55–7, 59,60, 64, 78, 85, 108

Balbo, Cesare   6, 23,30
Berlusconi, Silvio   114
Bismarck, Otto Von   8, 47, 85
Bologna   18, 20, 21
Bourbons (see Naples)
Brigands War, the   88–9
Buonarroti, Filippo   26

Calatafimi, battle of (1860)   71
Carbonari   20, 22
Castelfidardo, battle of (1860)   75
Cattaneo, Carlo   34
Cavour, Camillo Benso di   7, 8, 10,
   24, 30, 39, 44–65, 70–4, 76–80, 84,
   87, 89, 90, 92, 95–99, 114

Charles Albert   17, 23, 28–30, 33–4,
   36–7, 42
Charles Felix   20
Christian Democrats   111–3
Church (see also Papacy)   13, 22, 45–6,
   87
Communists   111–3
Craxi, Bettino   113–14
Crimean War   39, 47–9, 52
Crispi, Francesco   105–7
Croce, Benedetto   99, 100
Custoza, battle of (1848)   34
Custoza, battle of (1866)   85

D'Azeglio, Massimo   46, 52, 57, 64,
   87, 89, 92, 95
Depretis, Agostino   105–6

Emilia   59, 61

Farini, Luigi   57, 59, 64
Fascism   98, 107, 109
Ferdinand I of Naples   15–16, 20
Ferdinand II of Naples   32–3, 35, 49
Ferrara   16, 30
Ferrari, Giuseppe   103
Florence   45, 59, 63, 85
France   8, 33, 35, 38, 46, 48–9, 54, 56,
   59, 64, 78
Francis II   73, 75
Franz Josef   51, 58

Gaeta   34, 73, 75
Garibaldi, Giuseppe   8–9, 21–22, 35,
   39, 45, 49–50, 55, 63, 65, 69–80,
   84–6, 92, 95, 97–9, 103, 114
Genoa   17, 70
Gioberti, Vincenzo   6, 23, 27
Giolitto, Giovanni   105–7, 109
Gladstone, William   3, 77
Gramsci, Antonio   99–100

Historiography   94–101

Italian (language)   12, 17, 87

Königgrätz, battle of (1866)   85

Legations see Romagna and Papal States
Lissa, battle of (1866)   85
Lombardy   15–6, 24, 33–4, 36–7, 51,
   58–9

Magenta, battle of (1859)   57,
Mack Smith, Denis   3, 46, 89, 100
Manin, Daniel   33, 49–50